OUTBOARD TROUBLESHOOTER

www.fernhurstbooks.co.uk

OUTBOARD TROUBLESHOOTER

Peter White

fernhurst
BOOKS

First published 1996 by Fernhurst Books,
Duke's Path, High Street, Arundel, West Sussex, BN18 9AJ, UK

Printed and bound in Great Britain

British Library Cataloguing in Publication Data:
A catalogue record for this book is available from the British Library.

ISBN 1 898660 23 9

Acknowledgments
This book is a tribute to my many former students, whose constant
questioning and bemused expressions following the removal of an
outboard engine hood, highlighted a need for it.

I would like to extend my thanks to a trio of qualified engineers at
Robert Owen Marine, Porthmadog, North Wales: Robert Owen for his
patience in poring over the written word; Malcolm Lane and Ian
Roberts for placing their hands in some of the photographs and
supplying invaluable practical advice on servicing.

My thanks also go to Malcolm Pannell at Noah's Ark Marine,
Chichester, Sussex for so willingly offering further advice.

The book is dedicated to my wife, Hilary Claire for her total support
and unending drive and enthusiasm which spurred me on during
many late nights.

All photos by Peter White and John Woodward except p2-3 and p6
Honda, p51 Chris Boiling.
Diagrams p13, 15, 17 & 26 courtesy of Motor Boat & Yatching, p14 by
Honda, p21 by Pan Tek and all others by Peter White.

Edited by Tim Davison & Jeremy Evans

Cover design by Simon Balley

DTP by Creative Byte

Printed and bound by Ebenezer Baylis & Son Ltd

The author at work. One small step for man.....

Peter White and his wife, Claire manage a mobile powerboat training unit specialising in seamanship and safety. They use a very wide range of craft and power units.

The office of Seafever (International) Limited is based in East Grinstead, West Sussex.
As a mobile training unit they operate on inland and coastal waters of the UK and are often working abroad.

Contents

Introduction

I am a regular user of outboard engines. I rely on them for my business, so when I stand at the wheel of a boat and insert the key in the ignition I expect the engine or engines to fire up immediately. And when they do I listen to the way they are running before casting off any mooring lines. If they play up I can usually identify the problem. I know whether I can correct the problem or whether to consult an engineer. Although I am mechanically minded and fully understand engines, I am not an engineer and at present do not propose to become one.

This book has not been written with the intention of replacing the technical knowledge found in a service manual; it is impossible to cover all the manufacturers or refer to specific engines. The material within this book is a generalisation of types, compiled specifically to assist boat drivers in understanding the 'lump' sitting behind them, enable them to carry out day-to-day maintenance and advise them when to call in an engineer.

For the troubleshooting section I have drawn on the experience of over 15,000 hours of powerboat teaching. For the technical content I have relied heavily on Robert Owen, a qualified marine engineer from Porthmadog in North Wales. If you also rely on an outboard engine this book will, I hope, give you the confidence to plan almost any trip in the knowledge that, should anything go wrong, you will be able to return safely to base.

Peter White

IMPORTANT NOTE
New engines usually carry a 12-month warranty, while a few extend over 24 or 36 months. Honda have an extended warranty of 60 months! By doing your own maintenance you could invalidate your guarantee. It is very important that you make certain the work is allowable under the manufacturer's warranty.

1 Choosing

Much of what you will read in this book is common sense. Car owners who understand and service their own engines will have little difficulty relating to their marine counterparts. But there are differences, crucial ones. There are also a few little hints which may seem obvious but, believe me, have saved even the most knowledgable outboard user from expense and danger.

Many people, and especially first time boat buyers, will find the task of matching the engine and horsepower to the hull confusing. Engine salesmen are not necessarily the best people to advise a customer on what he or she really needs. So, if it's a motor boat you seek, first establish why you want it and ask yourself what you are going to do with it. Fishing perhaps, waterskiing, cruising, racing, and is it solely for leisure or commercial use?

The requirements of a commercial user differ considerably from those of recreational users. The professional will rely totally on power. How often do you see the harbour master collecting his fees at the helm of a sailing dinghy? Sailing boats use an outboard as auxiliary power. Large powerboats with inboard engines sometimes use a small outboard as a secondary 'get-you-home' means of propulsion.

Outboard users range from fire-fighters to fishermen, all attracted by the outboard's ability to deliver large amounts of power for its weight. They are also easily accessible for servicing. The smaller outboards can be quickly swapped from one boat to another and even the larger engines can be craned off the transom for a major overhaul.

Outboards are amazingly versatile. In the third world they are clamped on the back of canoes and flat-bottomed boats for exploration, transport and supply. Where proper fuel is scarce, they'll fire them up on petrol, then run them on paraffin.

There was a time when the outboard engine had a reputation for being unreliable. Modern technology and development, I have found, have made them more reliable than many inboard engines.

Sailing club rescue boats make perfect use of the outboard's ability to provide rapid response in shallow water. The rigid inflatable makes recovery easy.

An outboard at work.

This ski-boat's hull will have been designed specifically for its role, a vital component in any balanced package of power, propeller and boat

Matching boat to engine

Not without good reason do boatbuilders put together balanced packages comprising hull, engine and even trailer. In most cases there is a choice of engine size for a particular hull – a minimum and maximum rating within safety guidelines. These recommendations should be strictly observed. No builder will risk producing a hull and engine package that proves unmanageable to the point of being dangerous.

I refuse to drive boats set up by people who don't understand the basic principles of power-to-weight ratios; boats which are unbalanced and incapable of being driven with confidence at speed because the risk of losing control is too great. These are very real dangers. Excess power also means excess weight: hulls have been known to break up, or refuse to turn one way. At full power they have been known to flip over backwards, or ride on their chine and capsize.

Hulls of similar length, but of different design and purpose, may well be fitted with different sized engines. The power recommended for one 5.5 m (18 ft) boat might be between 90 hp and 200 hp; on another 5.5 m craft between 75 hp and 115 hp. One may be designed for speed, the other for cruising.

Rating

The horsepower rating of modern engines is taken from the propeller shaft of the gearbox and is usually calculated at maximum rpm, after the machine has been 'run in'. Engines built prior to the early 1980s are rated at the engine and the figure may be much higher. An older-style 50 hp is now rated at around 42 hp. You should not be surprised, therefore, to see a new, top-of-the-range 50 hp outperforming an older 60 hp model.

Buying secondhand

Before buying I would recommend running the serial number back through the computer records held with the manufacturer. He will inform you when it was built. In my view there is no justification for a vendor telling you, 'I don't know when it was made, but it's quite new!'. It's quite common to find a secondhand boat offered with its previous, and sometimes useless engine. Its more modern engine will have been transferred to the new hull. (See Chapter 10: Buying Secondhand.)

An outboard as small as 2hp will be quite powerful enough for a small yacht's tender and can be unshipped easily and stored away on passage.

How a two-stroke internal combustion engine works

A two-stroke engine combines induction, compression, power and exhaust into one revolution of the crankshaft or two strokes of the piston. There are no inlet or exhaust valves; instead the flow of fuel/air mixture is controlled by the movement of the piston itself.

1. As the piston rises fuel/air mixture is drawn from the carburettor, through the reed (non-return) valve, into the sealed crankcase. At this stage, the transfer and exhaust ports are blocked by the piston, so the previous charge, already in the combustion chamber, is compressed.

2. As the piston approaches the top of its stroke the compressed mixture is ignited, driving the piston down on its working stroke. The downward movement of the piston builds up pressure within the crankcase.

3. Towards the bottom of its stroke the piston uncovers the exhaust port, letting the burnt exhaust gas out of the cylinder.

Shortly afterwards, it uncovers the transfer port, allowing the new charge to flow into the cylinder from the crankcase.

4. The incoming charge helps push the exhaust gases out of the cylinder – a process known as scavenging. No matter how carefully the engine has been designed and built, it is impossible to prevent some mixing of the new charge with the exhaust. This affects efficiency, hence two-strokes' thirst for fuel. But it is also the key to the two-stroke's ability to produce a power stroke on every revolution, hence its high power/weight ratio.

Today's technological advances in the performance and economy of outboard petrol engines makes for a very quiet and smooth delivery of power. The latest generation is also cleaner, using and burning less oil for lubrication and the engines are more economical, using less fuel per mile than older ones. They reflect the world of today, where our resources require careful use and our environment needs protecting

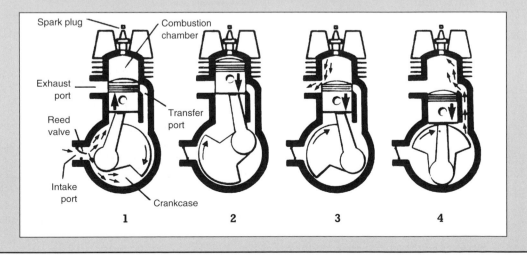

Spark plug · Combustion chamber · Exhaust port · Reed valve · Transfer port · Intake port · Crankcase

1   2   3   4

Power

One imperial unit of horsepower, hp, equals 550 foot-pounds per second. A foot-pound is the amount of energy expended to raise a weight of 1lb a distance of 1 foot, in this case in one second. One horsepower equals approximately 750 watts, or to be more accurate 0.7457 kW.

The commonest question I am asked is how the size of an outboard relates to its motor vehicle counterpart, in terms of cubic capacity or cc. Cubic capacity relates to the combined volume of all cylinders of an internal combustion engine.

Two-stroke outboards are internal combustion engines but we nearly always rate them in horsepower, not cc. A 200 hp outboard will roughly equal a 2.6 litre, or 2600 cc engine.

A litre is a metric unit of capacity, strictly the volume of one kilogram of water, about one and three quarter pints of water. A litre equals 1000 cc.

The larger two stroke engines need approximately 13 cc for each 1 hp they develop in power. A 75 hp outboard engine is about the size of a 1000 cc car engine. The smaller engines of around 2 hp, 4 hp and 5 hp have about 25 cc to for each 1 hp they develop.

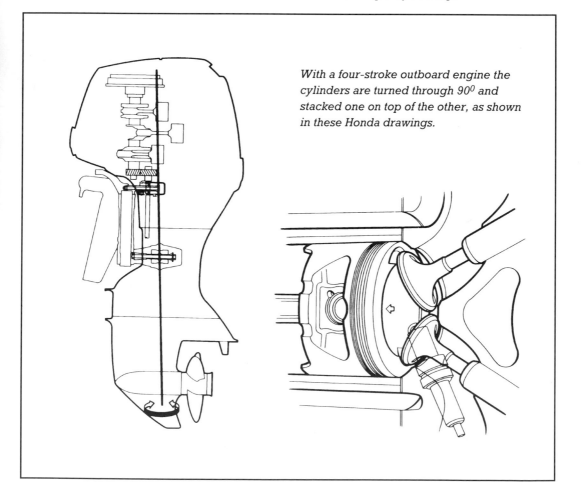

With a four-stroke outboard engine the cylinders are turned through 90⁰ and stacked one on top of the other, as shown in these Honda drawings.

2 Attaching the Engine

If the engine is not firmly attached to the boat, much of the content of this book will be irrelevant. (Alternatively, see the section on swamping!) Outboards can and do jump off the backs of boats because a few simple, commonsense precautions have been ignored.

Small engines

Small engines are generally clamped onto the boat's transom by wingnuts or clamp screws. Use only hand pressure to tighten them because undue leverage can strip the threads off either the saddle bracket and/or the bolts. But do make sure they are tight

The engine may look secure but the threads may have become worn, slip back on themselves and the clamps will then loosen. The engine may then vibrate off the transom. After tightening the clamps, re-check them after 15 minutes running time and periodically thereafter.

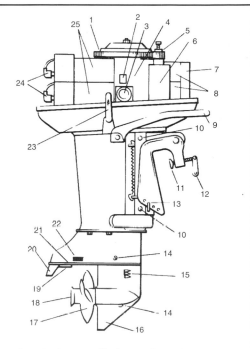

A typical two-cylinder outboard.
1. Flywheel; 2. Fuel Filter;
3. Fuel pump; 4. Crankcase;
5. Starter pinion; 6. Starter;
7. Air silencer; 8. Carburettors;
9. Carrying handle; 10. Swivel
brackets; 11. Transom clamps;
12. Locking holes; 13. Tilt adjustment;
14. Gearcase oil plugs; 15. Cooling
water inlet; 16. Skeg; 17. Propeller;
18. Exhaust through hub; 19. Anode;
20. Trim tab; 21. Anti-cavitation plate;
22. Cooling water outlet;
23. Gear shift; 24. Spark plugs;
25. Cylinders

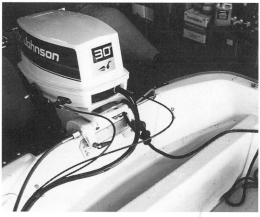

A lanyard, secured to engine and transom, will save embarrassment if the engine is dropped while lifting or vibrates loose of its own accord.

These clamp screws have been tightened hard by hand, then rechecked after 15 minutes' running. The anti-theft device on the right hand clamp is unfortunately vital these days.

Lastly, always tie the engine securely to the boat with a lanyard in case it jumps off the transom and every time you unclamp it or transfer it from boat to boat at sea. Always fix the engine as squarely as you can and at the correct height.

Larger engines

Large engines which are permanently fixed to the transom are invariably through-bolted, the top bolts often being protected with an anti-theft device. Depending on the type of installation, most are fitted centrally and squarely on the transom. Larger performance engines on small very fast hulls, however, may be shifted up and over to one side to compensate for the immense amount of engine torque they produce at full throttle.

The designers will have established where to drill the mounting holes. The major manufacturers will have got together with the boatbuilders to establish their correct position after sea trials. Templates will then have been made. The positions will differ from engine to engine and boat to boat.

The dangers of getting it wrong are real. There is the case of a boat and large engine combination that flipped when full power was applied. The hull twisted to starboard and

capsized. After a tiny modification, undetectable to the eye, the identical combination now has a superb record of achievement and safety. The importance of marrying up the correct components cannot be stressed too strongly.

While engines have been known to jump off transoms, a few transoms themselves have proved too weak to handle the power and have broken away. So the rule is, please, unless you know what you are doing, keep the size of the engine within the guidelines recommended by the manufacturer.

It is well worth obtaining expert advice for the final positioning and clamping of the engine. This should avoid your having to drill several different holes in the transom while attempting to find the correct location. Too many holes may terminally weaken the transom which carries, remember, not only the engine but also transfers its power to the hull. Plug and seal any surplus holes.

Long and standard shaft

Most transoms are designed for a long shaft engine. This leaves more height from the water level to the top of the transom. It follows that there is less chance for the waves to break over the stern, perhaps swamping the boat. A few specialised hulls have a low transom.

If a long shaft were fitted to a low transom the propeller would be too deep in the water. The engine would probably operate but its efficiency would suffer and excessive fuel would be used trying to drag the lower unit through the water. Again, if a standard shaft engine were clamped to a transom requiring a long shaft the propeller would be too high, and cut through air and water, possibly causing long term damage. The propeller must operate in the clear uninterrupted flow of water found just below the hull.

The difference between a long shaft and a standard shaft is 5 in (125 mm). The transom

Note that the anti-cavitation plate is at the same level as the bottom of the transom (hull).

height should be around 15 in (383 mm) for short shaft engines and 20 in (508 mm) for the long shaft. Extra-long shafts (25 in and 30 in are available.

For the best performance the anti-cavitation plate should be between 1 in (26 mm) above the bottom of the boat and level with the bottom of the boat. It is worth bearing in mind that a small adjustment to the height of the saddle bracket can be made by fixing a block to the top of the transom. This will lift the engine. Alternatively a small section of the transom can be cut away to lower it. Take care that any material removed does not structurally weaken the transom.

Where improved performance is required, large outboards are sometimes fixed to an extension bracket. This bracket must be very strong and may extend two or three feet, to lengthen the waterline of the boat. Because the engines are operating a short distance behind the hull they are running in the stern wave, which is higher than the water coming from the base of the hull. So the anti-cavitation plate is set much higher than for an engine mounted directly onto the transom. Some systems have hydraulic jacks to move the engines up and down vertically (not to be confused with trimming).

Control box

The engine control box serves several functions apart from acting as a gear selector and regulating the speed of the engine. On electric start engines it houses the ignition and choke switch. The key or button triggers the starter motor. It can also actuate the choke control which enriches the carburettor.

The control box links up various warning systems by either sound (horn) or light indicators. It has the switch for the kill cord

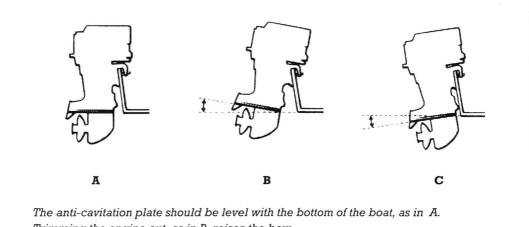

The anti-cavitation plate should be level with the bottom of the boat, as in A.
Trimming the engine out, as in B, raises the bow.
Trimming it in, as in C, depresses the bow.

Trim will make all the difference to ride and safety, but correct distribution of occupants' weight is essential for the boat to ride level at speed. Both these boats are out of balance.

connector for emergency stopping of the engine, and a fast idle lever to help start the engine when cold. It may also house the trim and tilt switch for engine angle adjustment. It also contains the wiring harness for instruments on the dashboard such as tachometer, hour-meter, trim gauges and speedometer.

When the control box is stripped down for the replacement of the control cables be careful to install the new cables the correct way round. If installed back-to-front, the gear lever becomes the throttle and the throttle becomes the gear shift! Obvious, really, but it has been known to happen. The cables must also be routed correctly for the safety of driver and crew. Avoid tight bends and kinks.

RUNNING IN A NEW ENGINE

This information has been taken from several different sources but all of them stress the importance of slow running for the vital first few minutes of an engine's life.

When demonstrating new engines, the sales personnel tend to drive them hard. It seems that potential customers are more interested in top speed and performance than the long life of the engine. The wear and tear of this high speed running on demonstration engines must take its toll.

My own engines have been run in

meticulously and two of them have logged over 2000 hours of trouble-free operation. This is despite the fact that they are used on training boats and constantly being stopped, started and taken through the gears.

My current engine is a four-stroke Honda. It's always been well maintained and, at the time of writing, was performing in an exemplary fashion. I put this down to careful running in.

The author's Honda 50 is a four-stroke which is more fuel-efficient and less polluting than a two-stroke. With regular servicing it should survive the rigours of its hard life for many years

The oil reservoir on a large two-stroke engine feeds a monitored amount of lubricant into the fuel, increasing it as the revs increase and vice-versa.

Alternatively, oil can be added directly to the tank. It is good practice to add the oil first and not to add a little extra for luck!

I firmly believe that reliability and longevity begin with the setting up and keeping to the initial running-in period, as recommended by the manufacturer. Thereafter stick to the correct fuel and oils, service regularly and work the engine through a variety of conditions, ie neither flat-out all the time, nor dawdling.

A general programme

The following is a general programme for running in a new engine which should cover most eventualities.

1. Ensure that the engine and fuel lines are matched correctly: the fuel tank and fuel lines must be compatible with the engine unit. The engine must receive the correct amount of fuel otherwise serious damage can occur. If the lines are too long between the tank and the engine or the fuel lines are too thin, the fuel pump will have insufficient strength to draw the correct amount of fuel.

2. Two-stroke engines require the recommended oil and correct grade of petrol. The fuel should be fresh and uncontaminated, particularly with water.

3. New two-stroke engines will require a double quantity of oil for the initial running-in period.

4. Where the engine has an automatic oil injection system it is obviously set correctly for the normal running of the engine. For the first few hours it will be necessary to double the quantity of oil by adding oil to the fuel. As a rule of thumb, the first two 5-gallon (25 litre) tanks of petrol require the double mix.

5. The quantity of oil is dependent on the normal running requirements of the engine. If the engine has a recommended 50:1 mix after the running-in period, it will be using a mixture of 15 oz of oil to every 5 gallons of gasoline (400 cc of oil to each 20 litres of gasoline).

While running in it will require a mix of 25:1. Double the oil quantity to 30 oz of oil to each 5 gallons of gasoline (800 cc of oil to 20 litres of gasoline).

The first 5-10 minutes

For the first few minutes operate at the slowest possible cruising speed or for the first ten minutes operate at fast idle only. Take care not to place the engine under an excessive load. This could happen, even at fast idle, if the design speed (displacement speed) of the hull was too low for the engine rpm. Running in a car engine below the recommended 4000 rpm up a steep hill in top gear is the easiest comparison that I can make.

Throttle back once the boat is on the plane for the first ten or so minutes of running and vary the speed until the engine is properly run in, a process which will take at least eight hours.

The next five minutes

Try and keep below 3000 rpm and vary the throttle settings after about ten minutes. If there is no tachometer and the boat has a lightweight planing hull bring her onto the plane and then reduce throttle power until she starts to come off the plane. At this point increase rpm very slightly and maintain this speed. Adjust the throttle settings after a few minutes.

The second hour

Continue up to around three-quarter throttle for short bursts (1-2 minutes) and then throttle back to about half maximum power to allow the engine to cool down. Remember to alternate the throttle settings during this second hour. Refer to manual.

NOTE:
Check the water jet tell-tale frequently. The double quantity of oil in the fuel will make it smoke. Slow running for long periods will oil up the spark plugs which will cause the engine to tick over in a lumpy and erratic fashion. This rough running should clear itself when the correct fuel/oil mix is used

The next eight hours

Continue running right up to the maximum rpm and keep changing the throttle settings every ten minutes.

The first 20 hours

This is the most important period when problems, if any, will occur. After the engine has been run for that period it will require a full check by the engineer. He will change the gear lube, check the timing and ignition, set the spark plugs, torque down the cylinder head screws, check the propeller, and adjust the carburettor and control cables.

TRIM TABS

The trim tab is a small vertical fin under the anti-cavitation plate above the propeller. It has a dual role: as a sacrificial anode to help combat galvanic corrosion, and to balance the steering, trimming out the tendency for the propeller throw to turn the boat one way or the other.

Before we delve into setting the tab we need to understand the way in which a hull behaves and why such a small piece of anode can so effectively 'tweak' the steering.

The trim tab will have an imperceptible 'set' which counteracts the prop's tendency to throw the boat to starboard. It also acts as a sacrificial anode to protect the engine leg from electrolysis. N.B. Not all trim tabs are sacrificial anodes. Some are only designed to fine tune the trim – these are usually painted the same colour as the body of the engine.

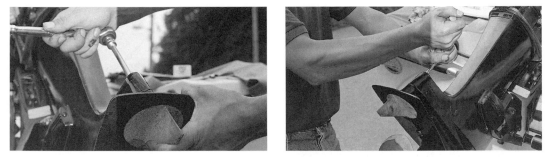

The trim tab is adjusted by slackening the nut above the anti-cavitation plate. If the boat turns more easily to the left (port), the trailing edge should be set a little to the left to compensate.

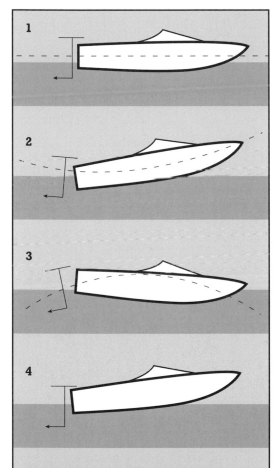

The ideal trim angle is found by trial and error.
Trimming up (2) raises the bow. Trimming down (3) depresses the bow. The ideal trim (4) allows the boat to plane perfectly.

This trim tab has been eaten away by electrolysis. Its protecting days over, it is also fairly useless as a trim tab and badly needs replacing.

Under the hull arc chines, also referred to as spray rails, ribs, ridges, or grooves. They run fore and aft to channel the water along the hull. They effectively create lift and give directional stability in cornering. They also help to keep the hull travelling in a straight line, preventing it from sliding and skipping.

When viewing an engine from the stern the propeller usually rotates clockwise when engaged in forward gear. This twisting action (torque) tends to want to twist the hull to the right (starboard) when trimmed in hard as in fig. 3. By balancing the boat and crew, by adjusting the trim mechanism (up and down) and by finding the correct power output, and setting the trim tab, it is possible to make the boat travel in a perfectly straight line. For a large twin engine installation, it is better for performance and balance to have the propellers rotating in

Trimming up pushes the bow out of the water, but the stern will dig in, causing drag. If the trim is correct the boat will fly and use less fuel.

opposite directions.

To discover the correct setting for the trim tab, first balance the boat by correctly loading crew and fuel, then bring the boat onto the plane on fairly flat water and trim up to free the hull from the water.Thus balanced, the controls should feel light to the touch. Now turn the wheel gently to the right and left. The steering wheel should feel light and the hull responsive. Wheel resistance should be the same each way. If this is the case, then the trim tab is set correctly. If there appears to be more resistance in one direction than the other, the trim tab needs re-setting.

If the wheel turns more easily to the left, position the trailing edge of the trim tab a little more to the left. If it responds more easily to the right, position the trailing edge of the trim tab a little more to the right. This may sound illogical, but it's correct. Try it.

Having set the trim tab – it will take trial and error – make a small dot punch mark under the anti-cavitation plate so that any replacement trim tab can be installed correctly. For a quick change, a felt tip pen will do.

As the trim tab is reduced in size by

electrolysis its effect as a steering aid will become diminished. If left unattended it can corrode away completely and give no clue at all to the correct position for its replacement.

When correctly balanced, try trimming down. The bow will drop and the boat will want to turn to starboard. It will now handle better when driving into the waves but will slow down and create excessive spray. Now start to trim up. As the bow lifts the hull will come back into balance. The speed will increase and the spray will reduce (less wetted surface area of the hull will be in contact with the water).

Porpoising

If you continue to trim up too far, the hull will want to turn to port. If the bow rises too high the bow will start to bounce or porpoise. Throttle back until the bouncing stops and then trim down. When the trim is set correctly, the bow will be just on the point of lift and fall. The hull is now set up for optimum speed.

With the trim tab set, the steering should be as light as a feather. The boat will then seek to fly, its hull subject only to the friction of air and water. But if the boat is heavy, out of balance, or the power unit is too small, the difference may not be discernible and the thrill will be lost.

3 Outboard Troubleshooting

This chapter is primarily concerned with troubleshooting, but first I felt it was only right and proper to explain how a healthy outboard engine should sound and behave if it is set up properly.

Starting procedure

Assume the usual considerations: that the engine has fresh fuel, is primed, the engine lower leg is down and in the water, the kill cord is attached to the helm and connected to the controls, the gear lever is in neutral, the accelerator lever is raised and the manual choke is in the on position (or the automatic choke ready to be engaged by a either a button or the starter ignition key).

Then turn the ignition key. After a few seconds the engine should start. As soon as it comes to life, turn the choke control off. With the choke off the rpm will rise instantly, so drop the throttle lever down and run the engine at around 2000 rpm for a couple of minutes. At the same time see if the telltale is spurting a strong jet of water.

When the engine is warm enough to run at idle speed without stalling, drop the accelerator lever down completely. The engine should now tick over on idle at around 800–900 rpm. The engine should not shake, splutter or cough and should have a regular, smooth beat.

Next, with the accelerator lever down, make a positive movement with the gear-shift lever into forward. A dull clunk should be heard as the teeth of the dog clutch engage and engine power is transferred through the gearbox to the propeller. Depending on the size of the engine

The gear lever and throttle are combined. Pushing forward engages ahead and increases revs, pulling back engages reverse and increases revs.

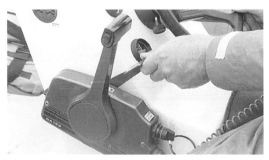

The small lever allows the driver to rev the engine in neutral for starting and warming up.

The kill switch instantly disables the ignition if the driver is thrown clear of the boat. It is not macho to drive without one attached to you.

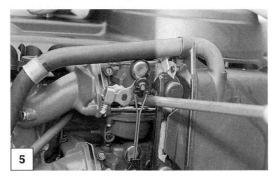

A journey round my four-stroke Honda.
1. A masterpiece of compact engineering;
2. The gear linkage;
3. Throttle linkage;
4. Throttle linkage at the carburettors;
5. The carburettors;
6. The fuel pump;
7. The dipstick.

the rpm may drop a little, possibly by as much as 100 rpm. Progressively move the accelerator lever forward. What follows should be an unhesitatingly smooth response of acceleration and the top end rpm should be reached quickly. (For most engines the maximum revs will be around 5400 rpm.) Gently pull back on the accelerator lever and return to neutral. The engine should be idling as smoothly and quietly as it was before the test run.

Now switch off and restart by using either the key or the hand-pull. It should start first time without the use of the choke or accelerator. Next, from neutral, move the gear lever smoothly and decisively into astern (reverse). Because the teeth in the gearbox are idling in forward mode the reverse gear engages with a fairly loud clunk. It's seldom as smooth as engaging the forward gear.

If you drag the lever slowly backwards into gear instead of being positive with it, the gearbox will make a horrible noise as the teeth

fail to engage and slip across the top of the teeth of the cogs. (Same effect going into forward gear.) Damage will be caused to the gearbox if time is spent dawdling between the neutral position and the gears.

As the power is applied, the take up on reverse should be as smooth as the take up in forward. Do remember that 3500 rpm in reverse is about the maximum.

Excessive speed astern will take the rear of the boat downwards as the flat transom builds up a wall of water which can cascade inboard and cause swamping.

An engine that is correctly tuned and in tune with the boat is a pleasure to use. Please follow the manufacturer's guidelines as set out in the operating manual. Finally, remember that keeping within the maximum recommended engine revolutions ensures the greatest engine efficiency, economy and longevity.

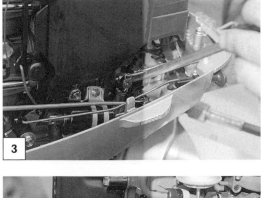

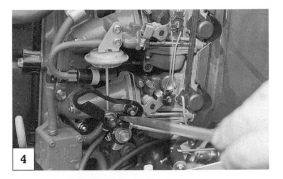

SUMMARY

A healthy engine should:

1. Start first or second time, after a receiving a few seconds burst of the starter motor.

2. Start within three pulls when using the hand pull-cord and, when warm, run smoothly and idle at around 800-900 rpm.

3. Have a smooth regular beat with a strong jet of water, although two-cylinder engines do usually sound a bit rough on tickover.

4. Make a dull clunk as the gear is engaged, with a small rpm reduction on tickover.

5. Have a smooth takeup of power from low rpm right through to the top end – no hesitation, no flat spots.

6. Reach top end rpm quickly, and meet the manufacturer's recommendations and guidelines.

Finally, remember that maximum rpm is ultimately governed by the loading and the propeller size.

SIMPLE ELECTRICS

Outboard two-stroke and four-stroke petrol engines need to generate electricity to spark the plug for internal combustion to take place. The electricity has to be controlled and also converted for different uses, such as charging the battery and supplying power for lights and navigational equipment.

Spark plugs

The specification pages in your handbook give the recommended type of spark plug for your engine. Different manufacturers have different designations for equivalent plugs. It is very important that the recommended plug is used because the spark has to take place in the correct position inside the ignition chamber as the piston compresses the mixture.

Spark plugs have different lengths of thread

The spark plug gap should be checked every 100 hours with a feeler gauge (A) and set to about 0.8 mm (0.03 in) with a special tool (B). Never touch the central electrode. Engines with CD ignition may use a surface gap plug (C).

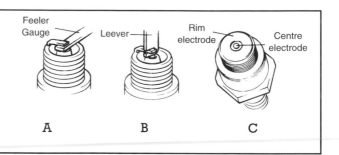

A   B   C

(referred to as thread reach). If, therefore, you use the wrong plug it could cause either too weak a spark, a spark in the wrong place or internal damage to the cylinder and/or head.

Plugs are made to operate at a temperature suitable for the engine. Symbols or codes stamped on the side of the plug relate to its heat range and other attributes. One symbol will refer to the construction of the plug, another to whether it is suitable for normal operation, racing use, or for a special application.

An engineer will analyse a spark plug in a similar fashion to a doctor trying to diagnose an illness. After first removing the plug, he will inspect the electrode (the firing end of the plug). The electrode acts like a stethoscope, supplying the engineer with information on the health of the engine.

The electrode of a normal plug, operating in the correct heat range with an engine correctly set up, will be coloured somewhere between light tan and grey, with no deposits. With surface gap plugs there will be a small deposit of similar colour around the top of each plug.

Do seek advice if the plug is damp, wet and very black with a strong smell of petrol. This could be the result of long periods of slow running or the engine being left on tickover. The fuel could be too rich or the two-stroke oil mixture too strong. It may be the result of an unsuitable spark plug working in the incorrect heat range (too cold).

The lower three plugs were removed from an engine that needed tuning. Compare with the three new plugs at the top!

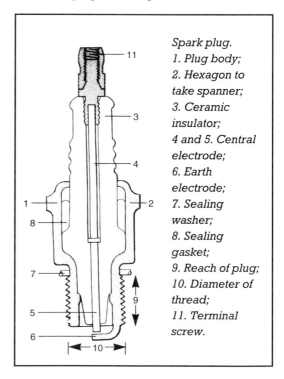

Spark plug.
1. Plug body;
2. Hexagon to take spanner;
3. Ceramic insulator;
4 and 5. Central electrode;
6. Earth electrode;
7. Sealing washer;
8. Sealing gasket;
9. Reach of plug;
10. Diameter of thread;
11. Terminal screw.

Overheating

If the plug shows bad erosion and very white deposits it is probably due to overheating. First check the heat range of the plug because it could be running too hot. If the plug is correct, check the following (details of how to do this are given later):

1. Timing.

2. Defective water impeller.

3. Partially blocked cooling passages.

4. Unsuitable propeller. (See Chapter 4: Propellers.)

Do not use the engine if:

1. There is a build-up of aluminium deposits around the firing end of the plug. This is due to excessive heat where metal has melted and adhered to the plug. This metal has come from the inside of the engine. The probable cause is pre-ignition and so it will not be remedied by replacing the plugs.

2. Deposits are welded to the spark plug through possible use of wrong oils or incorrect mixture, or incorrect use of the engine (do not confuse with 1, above).

The alternator is under the flywheel which, in this four-stroke Honda, is connected to the camshaft by a timing belt.

The condition of the spark plug is important to the engineer when attempting to find the cause of a problem. If you have tried to sort out a problem by replacing with a new plug, do keep the old one for the engineer.

Engines fitted with a battery

A battery supplies the electricity to spin the engine starter motor and also a secondary power circuit to operate lights, radio and other equipment. Once the battery has been used to start the motor, the charging circuit inside the engine replaces the electricity used, trickle charging it back into the battery.

Once the engine is turning it generates its own electricity. All the time it has fuel and it is running it is a completely self-contained unit.

Engines without a battery (recoil/manual start)

If the engine has no battery the initial electricity to spark the plugs will come from pulling the hand pull-cord at the top of the engine. With one positive pull it is possible to generate enough spark to fire the engine at least four, and maybe six, times.

Primary circuits

The electricity comes from an alternator under the flywheel on top of the engine. Magnets attached to the inside of its rim rotate around the

The alternator is under this flywheel. Note the handpull cord in place.

The coils momentarily store the enormous energy required to spark the plugs.

The Honda features CD ignition, rather than an old-fashioned distributor. Fewer parts and more precise sparking are the benefits.

stator, or stationary alternating coils. The spinning magnets generate alternating current (AC) in the stator. The current passes through a rectifier so that direct current (DC) flows into, and is stored in, the capacitor charging coils until required.

These coils store the charge briefly, building up a very high amount of power. An on/off switch releases this stored power which is sufficient to jump the gap at the spark plug.

Another coil, referred to as the trigger coil, is situated under the flywheel. This also produces electricity, but at a very low power. The voltage from the trigger coil goes into the switch box. The switch box is similar to a light switch. At a certain timed point it releases a current to the ignition coil. The stored voltage is now discharged and causes a surge of very high voltage (around 40,000 volts) across the spark plug gap. The engine fires. Once the stored voltage has been discharged from the capacitor charging coils, the switch closes and the cycle begins again.

The trigger coil moves with the accelerator to advance and retard the timing of the spark. This must be tightly controlled because the spark is required at a particular time in the cycle of the engine. The engine rotates at a different speed depending upon the throttle position. Therefore,

the spark timing changes as the revs increase and decrease.

Secondary circuits

Some of the electricity from the stator alternating coil is passed through a rectifier to supply a direct current for the charging of the battery and to operate navigation lights and control panel lights.

On larger engines there should be a voltage regulator between the rectifier and the battery. The regulator controls the amount of electricity recharging the battery, without which it is possible, especially on high rpm, to produce too much electricity. This will cook the battery and/or burn out lights and navigation equipment.

A neat and tidy wiring system is essential for reliable boating. This one is a potential disaster area.

The starting gear cog engages the flywheel, zooming up its shaft under centrifugal force when the ignition key is turned. If the pinion shaft or cog are abused, they can seize.

It is easy to check whether a voltage regulator exists or is working properly by starting up the engine and switching on a navigation light. With the engine out of gear, tweak the throttle and watch the intensity of the light. If it remains glowing everything is fine, but if it lights up like a searchlight, then there is a problem.

Our main area of concern is the visual condition of the wiring. Check for breaks and loose connections. It goes without saying that all electrical connections must be clean, secure and lubricated, all wiring sound and without breaks.

Avoiding damage

It is important not to interrupt the electrical circuit while the engine is running. Damage may be caused if:

1. The rectifier is left connected when the engine is running and the battery is then disconnected.

2. The polarity on the battery is accidentally reversed by changing the cables, causing damage to the charging system.

3. The circuit is opened by a broken wire or a loose connection.

Most of the electrical maintenance requires special tools and testing equipment. Seek advice from an engineer.

Flywheel removal

Even the first-stage removal of the flywheel requires special tools to free the nut. Striking the flywheel with a hammer or flexing the flywheel when trying to remove it can cause the magnets to become loose or even fall out. If a magnet comes out of position when the engine is running it can break up the inside of the flywheel which will in turn damage other expensive components.

Starter motor

This responds to the ignition key. It comprises an electric motor fixed vertically against the body of the engine under the flywheel. When the key is turned to the on position, the motor spins the pinion shaft. The speed flicks or throws the starter cog up and into the outside teeth of the flywheel.

Problems are usually caused by lack of maintenance, for example:

1. If the pinion shaft and cog are abused or neg-lected the cog can seize and refuse to climb up the shaft and into the flywheel. The starter motor spins but the engine does not turn.

2. If, alternatively, the actual pinion shaft seizes, when the key is turned the motor will remain stationary. It will hum. If the electrical power is not interrupted it will quickly burn out the motor.

A dismantled starter motor showing the armature and the casing containing the magnets and brush assembly. Brushes may burn out after long use, but can be replaced cheaply.

The brush kit is separated from the case and replacement brushes fitted. Make sure they go in in exactly the right way and watch those springs.

Freeing the starter motor

Remove the engine cover and the flywheel protection cover. Ensure the engine cannot start by checking that the electrical supply is off, the key has been removed and there is no chance of accidentally starting the motor while you are working on it. Soak the cog and pinion shaft with releasing fluid and leave for several minutes.

With pliers or an adjustable spanner begin 'worrying' the spindle and cog back to life. They should then turn freely in your fingers. Turning the cog by hand in the correct direction should twist it up into the flywheel. Before replacing the covers lubricate the spindle and cog, using the correct grease.

Take care when replacing the flywheel cover as a few will only go back on at a particular angle in order to avoid the timing arrow. You are now ready for an attempt at starting.

If the starter motor is completely seized it will either need to be stripped down or replaced.

Sometimes they fail to respond to the ignition key because the brushes are worn. The unit will need to be removed from the engine and completely stripped down. The replacement brush set must be installed in an identical way to

the one which was removed.

Water circulation

The engine produces heat like any other internal combustion engine during operation. This heat needs to be controlled. Excessive heat can melt the engine, causing it to seize. Water continually circulating the engine through water ducts will remove any excessive heat. The flow of water is calculated to ensure the engine reaches and maintains a correct working temperature via the thermostat.

The visual indicator for water circulation is the tell-tale. This is a thin strong jet of water forced out at an angle from a small hole under the lip where the hood clips into place. If it becomes blocked by small particles of sand and mud it can stop pushing out water. The toolkit should include a small piece of wire for pushing up the pipe to clear any obstructions. You must be certain that the stoppage has been caused by a blockage of this kind, before continuing to run the engine. If a blocked outlet tube is causing the stoppage it is not too serious a problem because the rest of the cooling water will still be circulating the engine.

A water pump is installed above the gearbox

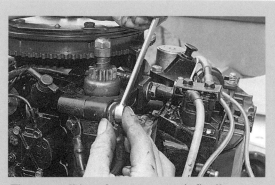

Once the starter motor has been checked and brushes replaced the armature is put back in the casing. The brushes are kept in place during the process by a special tool.

The reconditioned starter motor is finally bolted back against the flywheel housing.

A small selection of impellers and a housing.

The tell-tale is the visual early warning for the cooling system. If it is blocked, clear it with a piece of wire. If it is weak, check the water pump and impeller.

in the lower leg to keep the temperature correct. It is of the rubber impeller type (not self priming) and therefore needs to be submerged in the water in order to function. The engine must be lowered deep enough for the anti-cavitation plate to be under water.

There is usually a grid above the gearbox and under the anti-cavitation plate. This is the water intake grid for the pump. At the end of a session in salt water, the engine should be washed out with fresh water from a standpipe.

Slide the muffs (or ears) attached to the hosepipe over the water intake grid. Run up on fresh water for around five minutes to ensure the inside is thoroughly clean. (If the engine is not going to be used for some time, remove the fuel line and allow the engine to run dry of petrol.)

The impeller, enclosed in its body, is slightly offset from centre. As it spins it draws water into the pump through the inlet port, before forcing it out of the outlet port. The pipe that transfers the water up the shaft and around the engine is

The water pump is situated on this Mercury in the bottom leg. A new rubber impeller should be well greased before refitting to protect it during those vital first few seconds of use.

attached to the outlet pipe.

The water pump is connected directly to the drive shaft and spins with the engine. If the engine is started up out of the water it is vital that the muffs are in place and the hosepipe is turned on because the rubber impeller needs water for lubrication. There should be sufficient pressure for the tell-tale to squirt water. If after a few minutes there is no sign of water, stop the engine and check for obstruction. If there is still no sign of water I suggest lowering the outboard into a large dustbin filled with fresh water. If the engine runs dry it takes less than 30 seconds at 2000 rpm to destroy the impeller. I often tell the story of the young lad who was given an outboard as a present. In ignorance he invited friends around to see his engine. Having mounted it on a piece of garden furniture he started it up, revving it away madly and engaging the gears for some time. It eventually slowed down and stopped never to go again. The engine head had changed colour to a shade of brown and the moving parts inside had welded themselves together. The whole engine was seized. Surprisingly, he was unsuccessful in his warranty claim!

The first stage of freeing the lower leg. Remove the nuts using a ring spanner.

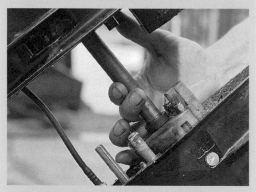

Carefully lever off the lower unit to expose....

... the drive shaft and gearbox linkage and the water pump casing.

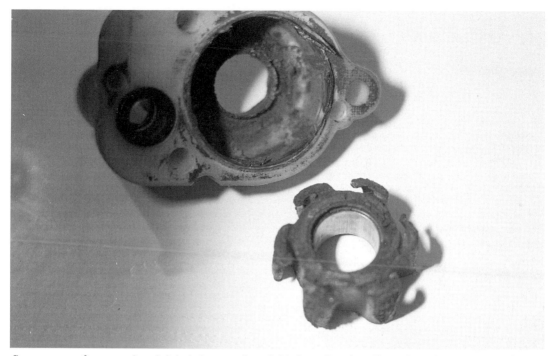

Severe wear from sand and debris has rendered this impeller virtually useless. The pump body looks in similarly bad shape and needs reconditioning before a new impeller is fitted.

In normal operation, if the telltale falters, switch off the engine and lift the leg to check for plastic bags or anything that could be blocking the intake grill. If the engine has been left in the down position for a long time it is possible that a family of small crustaceans may have taken up residence inside the grill.

Running the lower leg through mud and sand can also block the intake. As the impeller blades start to weaken and break down, the strength of the water jet diminishes and eventually becomes a dribble. It also takes longer to see the jet on start-up. It should normally be a strong stream of water.

In heavy weed, run slowly and stop often, reversing the drive to help kick off any weed. If you are in very heavy weed, stop, lift the engine and check the intakes before continuing. At the end of the run, check the water intake thoroughly.

If an electric sensor is fitted it will be at least two thirds up the engine block resulting in a delay before the pump can get water to this height when the engine is started. So sometimes an alarm signal sounds briefly when an engine is started after a long delay.

TWENTY COMMON PROBLEMS

Most problems are caused by a combination of a few common faults. Some of the symptoms are similar, but small differences dictate different remedies.

Problem 1
General starting difficulties

These could be caused by any one of the following:

1. Incorrect starting procedure. (Refer to handbook.)

2. Old, stale fuel. (Refer to Chapter 8: Fuel.)

3. Weak spark. (Refer to Chapter 3, section on electrics.) Change the plugs.

4. Water contamination. (Refer to Chapter 3, section on water circulation.)

5. Incorrect settings on carburettors. (Refer to Chapter 3, section on idle speed etc.)

6. Incorrect timing.

7. Some engines have a safety feature that prevents the engine from starting if it is out of the water, ie at an angle. Look to see if the engine is tilted too high, or this feature has developed a fault.

Starting checks
If engine will not start, check the following:

1. Starting procedure.
2. Battery and power.
3. Key.
4. Kill cord fitted.
5. Fuel in tank.
6. Fuel lines connected.
7. Primer bulb correct for direction.
8. Fuel in carburettors.
9. Fuel lines clear and not trapped.
10. Gear lever in neutral.
11. Enough choke (when engine is cold).
12. No choke (when engine is hot).
13. Fuel filter not blocked.
14. Fuel uncontaminated.
15. Fuel isnot stale.
16. Fuel/oil mixture is correct.
17. Spark plug leads are tight.
18. Spark plugs are tight.
19. Spart plugs have no faults.

Problem 2
The engine will not turn over

The battery is probably flat so check that:

1. The gear lever is in neutral. (You may need to waggle the lever to clear the safety cut-out.)

2. The power is turned on.

3. The battery is connected and the terminals are tight, clean and greased. If the battery is not the maintenance-free variety, check the fluid levels and top up with distilled water if below the top of the elements. If not, access the engine and:

4. Check the starter motor. It could be jammed. If it is, there is usually a humming sound. (See Chapter 3 – section on starter motors.)

5. Check the in-line fuse under the cover. If broken, replace with an identical one. It may have blown because the starter motor is jammed! (Fuses do not fail without a reason.) Please ensure the replacement fuse is compatible with the old one.

6. If the starter motor clicks and then makes a humming noise maybe it is engaging with the power-head but will not turn it. Remove the cover on top of the power-head and attempt a hand-pull start. If the engine turns by hand, the battery is probably too weak for the starter to spin the engine. Use the hand-pull method to fire up and once the engine is running it should restore power to the battery.

7. If the engine will not turn by hand or the starter motor is jammed, seek advice.

A battery problem is easily, if expensively, solved by its replacement. But before you do so, it may simply have been left for a long time and needs a thorough recharging.

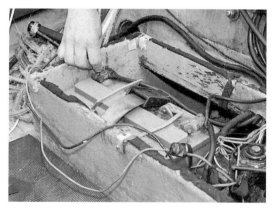

Check that the battery terminals are tight and greased. This may be the only reason for the engine's failure to turn over. In this photo the loose wires and sticky tape are dangerous.

The majority of large engines can be hand-pulled successfully.

Problem 3
The engine turns over on the starter but will not start

Work through the following:

1. Check the condition of the battery: it should be fully charged. The engine should turn over quickly. (See Chapter 3, section on electrics.)

2. Check that the kill cord is attached - it is often the most obvious item causing the problem.

3. Has the fuel line been connected? Both ends?

4. Is there fuel in the tank?

5. Is the engine in the down position?

6. Check that the fuel is in the carburettors - forgetting to prime the system is not unusual. If it still will not start maybe it is now time to look at the electrics.

7. Check the quality of the spark at the plugs. (See Chapter 3, section on spark plugs.) To do this you will need a plug spanner. Remove a spark plug and earth it. Wedge the plug against the engine and remove your hand. While one person looks for the spark give the engine a quick flick on the starter. Remember to fit the water muffs which allow you to run the engine attached to a hosepipe, or clamp the engine in a water tank. Do not start the engine without water to lubricate the water pump.

NOTE
You could use a plug spark tester, in which case the plug can remain in situ. If the spark is yellow it is weak and the engine will not fire. You need a strong blue spark.

8. Assuming there is a satisfactory spark, check

the quality of the fuel: it needs to be fresh. Fuel has a recommended shelf life and becomes stale after several weeks. Over several months it will not have sufficient octane to fire up an engine. Although I do not recommend sniffing the fuel, old fuel smells foul whereas fresh fuel has the whiff of a garage forecourt.

Make certain the tank is vented and the fuel line is free of kinks. Visually (if possible) check

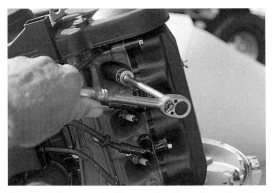

Prevent damage to the spark plugs by using the correct tool.

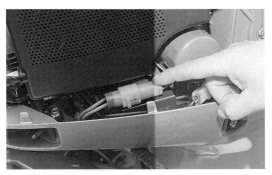

Removing the spark plug on a Honda. To check the spark remove the plug, wedge it against the engine to earth it (keep hands away) and turn the engine.

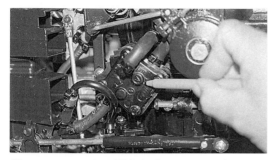

Know your engine. This is the same engine, a 1988 Mercury 75, showing the fuel line to the fuel pump; the white in-line fuel filter; the fuel pipe to the top carburettor and air-intakes for the three carburettors.

the tank for water. If water is present, it will have collected on the bottom in small globules and will then be taken through the fuel line/s to the carburettors. Now the problem really begins to become serious. The water will collect in the lower part of the float chamber and will eventually block the slow running jet: this prevents the engine ticking over at slow speed. Access the engine and remove the drain plugs at the base of each carburettor.

The fluid now draining out should be petrol. If it is, close off the drain plugs. If water drips/pours out you will need to squeeze the primer bulb, pushing fresh fuel into the system. The contaminated fuel in the tank requires changing or treatment: see the section on fuel in Chapter 8. With fresh fuel attempt a restart.

9. If the engine still refuses to start the jets in the carburettors may be blocked. An engineer should remove the carburettors and clean them.

10. Incorrect starting procedure. (Refer to handbook.)

11. Fuel tank contaminated. Empty the tank and put fresh fuel through the system. (See section on emergency starting.)

12. Pinched or restricted fuel lines.

Drain plugs on this Mercury's carburettor allow water and sediment to be drained off. If this doesn't do the trick, the jets may be blocked. Revving may clear them (see text).

(Easy to cure.)

13. Dirty or restricted fuel filter. Remove and clean.

14. Electric choke not operating. If your engine has a manual choke override, use it. Neither choke is required if the engine is already warm.

15. Inlet needle in carb stuck open, or closed. If open it will flood the carburettor with fuel.

16. Primer bulb could be restricting fuel flow. Inside the fuel line primer bulb there are two one-way valves, which prevent the fuel from running back down the line and into the fuel tank. If they break down they will not pump the fuel through when they are squeezed. Replace, arrow towards engine, or it may be possible to run the engine, once primed, without the bulb as a get-you-home measure.

Carburettors removed from a Mercury.

Problem 4

The engine can be started but it will not tick over and you suspect there is water in the system. Try this emergency start procedure

Start the engine and run up to around 3000rpm. Give it some choke, either electronically or manually. Leave it on until the engine nearly stalls and then let the choke off. The rpm will again build and when 3000rpm is reached, once again give it some choke.

This procedure will have starved the engine of air and because it was revving so high it will have pulled neat fuel through in place of the air (and possibly any rubbish that was also stuck in the carburettor jets).

Due to the air starvation the fuel could not ignite (engine was flooding) which is why the engine was stalling. As long as you let the choke off before the engine rpm becomes too low it will pick up as soon as there is a renewed air/fuel mixture to ignite. This has worked very well in the past with me and is a very quick and easy method in an emergency. It is not a long-term remedy as the original problem was contaminated fuel, which will need dealing with. (See Chapter 8: Fuels – section on fuel treatment.)

Problem 5

The engine will start but won't run

This could be due to:

1. Blocked carburettor jets. The engine will be running rough at, say, 3000rpm and as the throttle control is brought back to idle the engine shakes and stalls. Try clearing the carbs. (See Problem 4.)

2. Incorrect settings on the carburettor/s.

3. Air leaking into the fuel system, usually because the diaphragm in the fuel pump has become rotten and started to break down.

4. Possible breakdown of the gasket between carburettor and engine.

5. Some outboards have a cylinder head gasket and this can cause several different problems, one of which could prevent the engine from ticking over at slow speed.

The head gasket acts as a seal between the head and the cylinder block. If it breaks down it will either leak air or water into the cylinders. The water will turn to steam and the slow running on one of the cylinders will be seriously impaired. Hence the inability to tickover. There are other visual indicators such as a white spark plug.

The tell-tale water jet will be very weak or non-existent at slow speed. In place of water there may be steam. The exhaust gases from

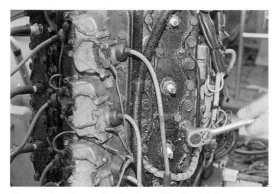

Removing the cylinder head bolts. Make sure you follow the correct order to avoid stressing the head.

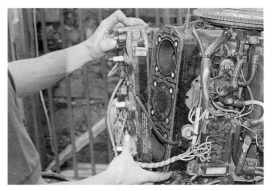

The cylinder head will lift off to show the cylinders. In the middle one the piston looks badly damaged.

This gasket will need replacing as it has been letting water into the cylinders. Water was also squirting out onto the starter motor, which seized.

This is the damage that can be caused by broken piston rings. The engine will need new pistons, rings and cylinder head and re-boring. Better still, scrap it.

the cylinder are being forced through the broken gasket into the water cooling passages. At slow speed the pressure from the water pump may not be strong enough to force the cooling water around the engine.

The amount of water in the system is reduced, so is unable to cool the engine which overheats (usually the top cylinders) and boils the water. Overheating does more damage to the gasket, cylinders and pistons. The steam inside the engine washes out the oil used for lubrication. This increases the friction between the moving parts, which in turn develops heat

and within a short while the engine will cook and eventually seize. (See Chapter 3, section on water pump and circulation.)

NOTE

Most modern engines have heat sensors and will automatically close down if overheating occurs.

Where there is no head gasket the engine head fits against the cylinder block, metal to metal, a perfect fit. If the cylinder head should crack the above symptoms can occur.

Problem 6
The engine overheats

Overheating occurs when the water cooling system breaks down or is impaired. This can be as a result of several small problems:

1. The impeller blades of the water pump have been damaged or are worn out. The water pump requires lubrication and relies on being immersed totally in water. It takes only a few seconds to burn out a dry impeller.

If you wish to fire up the engine to make sure it starts prior to putting the boat in the water, then the hosepipe and muffs must be attached and the water turned on before firing up. Or place the lower leg in a tank of water. Don't ever think you can get away without damage with just a quick spin on the starter motor. Every time you turn the engine, wear occurs on the dry impeller blades. Most outboards hit high rpm as soon as they fire up.

Some manufacturers recommend that the impeller is changed every season. I have run the same impeller for over a thousand hours and still had a very strong tell-tale. Obviously over a period of time the blades become weak and the suggestion of a yearly replacement is sound advice.

2. Blocked water intake. The lower leg must be immersed under water before starting the engine. If you always make sure the anti-cavitation plate is under water at least you are protecting the water pump. But the water intake grill must be clean and clear of weed, mud, grit and sand. If you leave the lower leg in the water weed and barnacles will grow inside the water intake which will prevent clear circulation of water. A stiff brush should remove most of the rubbish. Do not use a wire brush.

When under way check the tell-tale regularly. Plastic bags and seaweed can easily wrap around the lower leg causing poor or no water circulation. At speed the handling characteristics will change and you will probably hear and feel cavitation at the propeller. (See Chapter 4: Propellers – section on cavitation.)

The thermostat housing on the Honda. The thermostat regulates cooling water flow round the cylinder head, restricting flow when the engine is cold, increasing it when it warms up.

The temperature and oil pressure sensor on the Honda. They are linked to visual/sound warnings which actvate in good time for the driver to take action.

3. A fault on the thermostat can also cause overheating. If it jams closed it won't allow full circulation of coolant . Replace thermostat. (See Chapter 3 – section on water circulation.)

4. A fault on the electronic heat sensor can indicate a false heating problem. Feel the temperature of the tell-tale. If it is still cool, slowly run back to base, checking continually. If very hot, or if steam is emitted, close down the unit and organise a recovery tow.

5. It is a very common occurrence to run up the engine and discover no tell-tale. First check that the tell-tale jet is unobstructed. Small particles of sand/grit/salt and even crustaceans can block the hole. Always carry a small piece of Monel seizing wire. If that doesn't do the job, remove the hood and carefully remove the tube from where it exits through the casing and clean the jet. With the hood off and the tube disconnected, start the engine. Hopefully a strong stream of water will emerge. Refit the tube and continue.

A strong stream of water from the tell-tale indicates that all is well in the cooling system. A blocked pipe can confuse matters. Poke it with a bit of wire before dismantling.

Problem 7
No water circulation

This could result from:

1. Impeller not working.

2. Blockage.

3. Tell-tale blocked.

(Refer to Chapter 3 – section on water circulation.)

Problem 8
No acceleration or poor acceleration

This can result from a range of problems and I will try to identify as many as possible. They are not in any particular order of importance and most will cross-reference with other sections in the book.

1. The engine is unsuitable for the type and weight of boat.

2. It is incorrectly propped.

3. The propeller is damaged.

4. The engine is incorrectly installed.

5. There is an obstruction around the propeller.

6. The boat is overloaded.

7. The weight in the boat is wrongly distributed and therefore the boat is out of balance.

8. The hull is carrying weed and barnacles.

9. Osmosis. Water penetrating the GRP hull usually only affects boats left for long periods in the water. The weight of water absorbed can be greater than the weight of the hull when new. Hulls can be protected and you need to speak to a reputable boatyard for advice.

10. Fuel starvation. One of the simplest and most common reasons for poor acceleration is a closed air vent valve on the fuel tank. The fuel pump on the engine can only suck against a certain amount of pressure (vacuum). On really large engines I have seen metal fuel tanks bend inwards and plastic tanks collapse completely. If you are really unlucky the vacuum can destroy the non-return valves in the primer bulb.

The key symptom of this is the power slowly dropping away over a few hundred metres. When you check the systyem you will find the primer bulb flat. Release the air vent, prime the engine and return to normal running.

11. Sometimes the air vent is open, the tanks are full of fuel and the tickover and takeup of acceleration are acceptable. But as soon as full power is asked for the engine seems to be held back and in some cases can die completely.

The cause could be:

A. The fuel line has too long a run from the tank to the engine.

B. It is too narrow a diameter to supply fuel in the required quantity.

C. The fuel outlet fitting in the built-in tank has too small a diameter or has been designed with 90^0 bends thereby restricting the flow of fuel.

D. The in-line fuel filters need cleaning or changing.

E. The fuel line is trapped or kinked.

F. The fuel is stale or contaminated in the tank.

G. The fuel pump diaphragm is weak and unable to pull the fuel through in sufficient quantity.

I have also come across a problem identified as a 'fuel starvation syndrome' in which the power falls off as soon as full throttle has been applied. The unit was checked twice without finding any faults. The frustrated engineer, determined not to be beaten, took the boat out onto the water and found that the propeller was pitched too small. When the power was applied the engine rpm went over the top of the band and the rev-limiter cut in. The inexperienced helm identified the cause as fuel starvation and had complained bitterly about the bad service he had received from the engineer. The engineer in question had not supplied or fitted the engine.

H. Finally, carburettor advance and retard settings could be incorrect. Seek advice from the engineer.

Problem 9
The engine stalls in neutral

As you move the lever from ahead to reverse (or vice versa) the engine stalls and you drift into another boat or mooring. It only takes a few seconds at the mercy of the wind and tide to put the manoeuvre and the boat in jeopardy.

The power unit must be able to tick over smoothly at around 800rpm. Any higher and the gearbox starts to take excessive punishment when engaging gears. The solutions, most obvious first, are:

1. The engine is not up to temperature prior to driving away and it will not tick over. In UK waters I run up at around 2000 rpm for about three minutes and longer for large engines. In warmer climates the unit can often be driven away as soon as it is running.

2. The fuel tank vent is closed.

3. The tickover (idle setting) is set too low.

4. The idle jet in the carburettor is blocked.

5. The fuel is contaminated, usually by water and fuel deposit – it looks like very fine sand or sludge.

6. The fuel is old and stale.

7. There is air leakage in the fuel system.

8. An incorrect mixture of air and fuel is being supplied to the spark plug.

9. There is a suspect plug – change plugs.

Setting the tickover idle speed

An engine out of water and running on its muffs and hosepipe should tick over at a higher rpm, say 1200rpm, than when it is in the water. As soon as it is in the water and set at the correct depth it will tick over at around 800rpm. This is because there is back pressure of water in the exhaust chamber.

Most exhaust systems push most of the fumes out through the centre of the propeller. At rest the water will have filled the inside of the lower leg up to the water level of the sea. When firing the engine, this water is forced out of the lower leg through the exhaust exit at the propeller.

The most efficient method of setting slow tickover (idle) is to put the boat in the water, engine down in the normal position and loaded with gear, fuel and crew. The extra weight of the engineer lying over the stern with his screwdriver lowers the stern that little bit more. Now set the idle speed. As soon as the engineer climbs out, the idle speed rpm will be a bit higher. This is useful for reversing because then the stern sinks lower, reproducing the conditions when the idle speed was set. This prevents a stall when reversing

10. The engine has been running at tickover too long and has oiled the plugs, preventing a strong spark.

11. An oversized engine (which is too heavy for the boat) is too low in the water, preventing the exhaust gases from escaping. This is the only occasion I can think of when the inability of the engine to tick over is beneficial. If the boat were to drive away fast it would probably flip over backwards and disappear in a cloud of spray.

Adjusting the idle screw on a bank of three carburettors. It's best set by dangling over the stern and adjusting with a screwdriver when the engine is warm. The tickover will rise a little when the weight comes off (see text).

Problem 10
The sneeze or cough

These are the most descriptive words I can use for a common fault at tickover which sometimes causes smaller engines to stall. Most large engines can sneeze/cough on one cylinder while the others fire normally and override the problem.

The symptoms are that the engine ticks over quietly, maybe for some time, and then sneezes, shudders and falters before resuming normal tickover until the next sneeze. This can be caused by:

1. Incorrect fuel/air mixture on the carburettor settings.

2. The reed valve being stuck open or partially damaged, allowing the fuel to blow back into the carburettor.

The reed valve is operated by the alternate vacuum and pressure caused by the piston sliding backwards and forwards in the cylinder. As the piston moves towards the spark plug it sucks fuel and air through the reeds. When the piston returns in the direction of the carburettor the pressure closes the reeds preventing the fuel/air mixture from being blown back through the carburettor. The exhaust gases are forced out and down a side chamber.

If the reed fails a sneeze results, sometimes referred to as a backfire. Technically it cannot truly backfire because the fuel/air mixture is not in a combustible state, ie under pressure in an explosion chamber. (See the earlier grey panel in Chapter 1 on how the engine works.)

Problem 11
The engine shakes its head

If the engine runs very rough on tickover and continually shakes its head the cause can be an ignition timing fault. It is best to get an engineer to check the ignition advance settings.

> *Important notes on slow and difficult engine tickover*

When an engine fails to tick over on idle but will run at higher rpm, or ticks over in a lumpy way and stalls when the gear is engaged, it is possible in an emergency to catch the engine before it stalls. Assuming the engine runs at a reasonable speed out of gear, drop the accelerator lever and engage the gear as the rpm reduces to around 1200 rpm. Catching the engine at around this speed should prevent it from a complete stall. As the gear is engaged accelerate and the engine should respond. The crunch on the gearbox and the jolt on the engine mounting bushes (saddle and swivel bracket) is an indicator of the serious damage that could be done if this were to become normal working practice. In fact, with an older engine this might be all that is required for metal to part company. Replacement gearbox components are very expensive!

> *NOTE*
> *EMERGENCY ONLY. This is not recommended as it could damage the engine, but it may get you home*

Problem 12
The engine is flooded with fuel

The engine won't fire if it is flooded. This is caused by excessive pumping of the bulb, or the float jet in the carburettor being stuck open.

Flooding is also sometimes caused by failing to adhere to the starting sequence. Maybe the kill cord was not attached while the engine was being turned over by the starter motor, or the pull-cord was not given enough energy.

I have also seen this problem arise when the weather was very cold and the engine was started on the muffs for a few seconds without allowing it several minutes to warm up. It was then put into the water where it failed to respond.

If you have the time leave the engine alone for about ten minutes when the excess fuel will drain or evaporate away. A re-start should be possible. Alternatively, try either or all of the following:

1. Disconnect the fuel line. Don't take the kill cord off, or no electricity will go to the plugs.

2. Remove a plug and make sure it is correctly earthed to the engine and away from the excess fuel. The spark can jump about 30mm. If the plug is not earthed or is allowed to slip, serious damage can be done to the electrical system. For safety it takes two people – one to crank over the engine by hand or by starter and the other person to hold a clean rag over the plug hole. As the engine is cranked over, the piston forces out the excess fuel. The rag should absorb the petrol. Otherwise the fuel will spurt out dangerously.

Repeat with all the cylinders and then, after replacing the plugs, attempt the correct starting procedure.

3. Drain down the carburettors.

4. If the problem is a stuck float jet, drain down the carburettors and start up. The fuel in the system should run long enough to pull through any dirt in the jets. If you get the engine running put the choke on for a brief moment. Replace the fuel line to the engine, prime and re-start.

Problem 13
Excessively high idle speed
(eg 1200 rpm instead of 800 rpm)

Assuming the engine was originally running at the correct speed in idle, the most common reason for a higher than normal tickover is that the cable controlling the acceleration has become worn or dirty and is sticking. In other words when the throttle lever is placed in neutral the cable under the hood has not returned to its correct position.

Do look at the cables before trying to find fault with the idle setting screw on the carburettor/s.

With the engine stopped remove the hood and ask your colleague to move the acceleration lever only, up and down. When in the idle position the lever should be resting on a stop. If it is not seated correctly just move it back and forth with your hand and check for movement. A spray with freeing oil may cure the problem. In other cases the screw adjustment may need resetting.

If the problem is not the accelerator cable:

1. The carburettor settings may be stuck open.

2. The reed valves may be chipped or broken. (See section on fuel systems.)

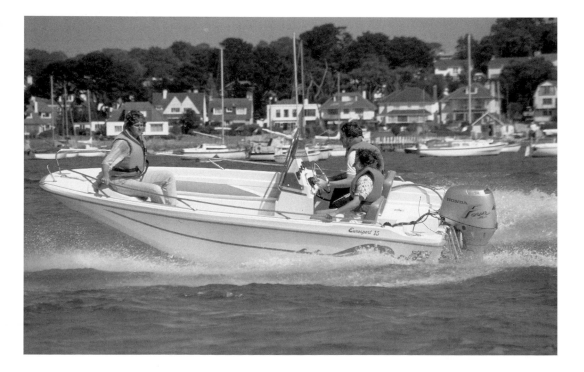

Problem 14
Pre-detonation (premature combustion of fuel)

Pre-detonation is the ignition of unburned fuel/air mix before the spark plug has fired. Also known as pinking, pinging, plinking and knocking, it is often caused by low octane fuel and if you refer to Chapter 8: Fuel, most of this will be explained.

Because the explosion is very slightly out of sequence it sends stress waves through the engine. After a time it can create havoc with the pistons and piston rings sending shock waves into the bearings. Obviously it will find or create weaknesses within the engine.

Another cause of pre-detonation is to operate an overloaded boat, when the engine rpm will be too low. (See Chapter 4: Propellers.)

Boats that are correctly propped for normal running will not be balanced if used for towing, unless the driver keeps the rpm to a minimum and maintains displacement speed.

Pre-detonation could be caused by:

1. Incorrect type of spark plug, running too hot.

2. Excessive fuel.

3. Engine running too hot, water not circulating correctly.

4. Fuel-to-air mix too weak at or near maximum rpm.

5. Low octane fuel or stale fuel.

6. Incorrect propeller: pitch too high, engine unable to reach maximum rpm.

7. Carbon deposits in the cylinders and on the pistons, increasing the compression ratio.

Pre-detonation can normally be prevented by setting up the engine properly in the beginning, followed by correct maintenance.

The electrical setting on the advance and retard can make for detonation even though all other factors are correct. If it is too far advanced, the spark on the plug will occur too soon for the position of the piston. (See Chapter 3 – section on electrics.)

Tuning notes

As the piston moves up the cylinder towards the spark plug, a mixture of petrol and air is compressed (see Chapter 1 – how an engine works). This highly combustible mixture is ignited by the spark in a controlled explosion which forces the piston back down the cylinder. Therefore it is very necessary for the compression within the engine cycle to be correct so the unit develops the correct power output. A lower compression in one or more of the cylinders will stop the engine from being correctly tuned-up, also preventing it from reaching its peak performance. Fuel consumption will also be high.

If the powerhead shows signs of overheating, such as scorched, blistered or discoloured paint, the engine must be looked over by an engineer. He will remove the plugs and fit a compression gauge in the spark plug hole. The engine is cranked over several times and the highest reading taken. Variation between cylinders should be within approximately 15lb/sq in. Anything greater indicates a defect that should be remedied before tuning can take place.

Obviously he'll need to check the cooling system and that the recommended type of two-stroke oil is being used! Using non-recommended fuels can cause overheating and permanent engine damage.

Weather conditions affecting performance

The weather plays a very important part in the efficient running of an internal combustion engine. All engines are horsepower rated under a controlled test standard (ISO3046). The data is obtained by a dynamometer (an instrument for measuring energy expended). The results of the tests are corrected for sea level using standard atmospheric pressure of 29.61 inches of mercury (1013.2 millibars or 1 atmosphere or 14.7 lb/sq in).

The results are also adjusted for an air temperature of 25 degrees C and a relative humidity of 30 per cent. The horsepower rating is now set.

A change in weather conditions will directly affect the performance of an internal combustion engine. Power is reduced in the summer if temperatures are high and atmospheric pressure is low and the humidity (water vapour) content high. The result is a slight decrease in boatspeed. It has a knock-on effect: because the speed is lower, the propeller does not reach its recommended rpm. We now have even less speed from the combined effect of air quality and too large a propeller for the conditions.

The performance of an internal combustion engine will vary according to the density, temperature and pressure of the air. It is therefore very important to tune the engine to the boat with a propeller that allows the engine to reach maximum rpm with a wide open throttle while being fully loaded. The engine will operate in an rpm range which is compatible with most conditions while reducing the possibility of pre-detonation. The engine will be more reliable and have a longer life, and spend less time in the workshop.

Problem 15
Starter solenoid jammed

The ignition key (or starter button) on the console (or dashboard) can only handle 12 volts at low amps. The starter motor requires full power from the battery, so the key simply triggers an in-line switch (starter solenoid) capable of handling the very high amps the starter needs.

When the key is turned an electromagnet in the solenoid is activated and a heavy plate closes the contacts. The electrical circuit from the battery to the starter motor is now complete. When the engine has started up, the key is allowed to return to the neutral position. Without electricity to the solenoid, the magnet drops back taking the connecting plate with it. Without power the starter motor stops and disengages itself from the flywheel.

A very long burst of power to the starter motor can overheat it and burn it out. It also drains the battery very quickly. A healthy engine only requires a quick flick of the ignition key to start it running.

A jammed solenoid will open the circuit to the starter motor which will stay open even when the ignition key is turned off. The starter motor will run continually until it burns out or drains the battery.

If the engine has already fired up, you will hear a high pitched whine from the starter motor because it will probably be running free. The only quick cure is to switch off the engine and disconnect the battery immediately. Do not leave the engine running when the battery is disconnected as it will damage the charging circuit.

A jammed solenoid will need replacing. It may be possible to free off the electromagnet by a gentle tap on the side of the solenoid which may free off the connecting plate from the contacts. Only on re-connecting the battery will you know whether it has been successful. In any case it will surely stick again and could cause serious damage.

Rev limiters

Most modern engines have a safety cutout system that prevents the engine from exceeding a maximum rpm set by the manufacturer. It simply keeps the engine running within defined top end limits. Depending on the way in which it has been installed it may reduce power or close the unit down.

It may cut in if:

1. The propeller is too small for the unit.

2. The engine is incorrectly mounted permitting excessive cavitation.

3. Ventilation occurs when under way.

4. The trim on the engine is too high, lifting the propeller clear.

5. The boat lifts off the top of a wave and becomes airborne

Rev limiters stop the engine overrunning when the propeller is out of the water, otherwise skilful throttle control is needed to avoid damage.

Emergency starting 1
With no electricity

Even if the battery is dead, keep it connected to the system. As soon as the engine fires it will generate an electrical current and if disconnected from the battery it may burn out the charging circuit.

WARNING

The control lever must be in neutral. If the engine starts while still in gear, serious injury or death can result.

Remove the head cowling protecting the flywheel and wind the emergency starting cord (in the only way possible) around the flywheel. The stopper knot in the end of the rope can only lock in one direction into the flywheel. Wind clockwise – about two turns.

Turn the key to the 'on' position and lift the accelerator lever. This will need to be closed down once it fires. If the engine is cold, and you have no electricity the automatic choke won't work. Push the manual override choke lever to 'on'.

NOTE

Keep your hands and fingers clear of the flywheel. Do not have loose clothes or scarves dangling. Balance your body to avoid falling overboard. Remember that when the rope has spun off the flywheel your body and elbow are in motion. Any person close by and behind you may be struck firmly by your elbow.

Try to keep your arms straight when pulling, in other words use the weight of your body to do the work.

The engine should fire after no more than three attempts. Once the flywheel is in motion it generates sufficient electrical power from the powerhead to run the engine without a battery (manual start).

Once the engine fires, flick off the choke and throttle back to around 1500 rpm. Now that the engine is running it will be putting electricity back into the battery.

Do not replace the powerhead cover. Do not replace the engine hood. Stay well clear of all moving parts.

With this method of emergency starting the engine can still be switched off by either using the key or the kill cord.

Many outboards, such as this Honda, will carry an emergency pull-cord in a neat little bag inside the hood

Wrap the starter cord round the flywheel and give a sharp, steady pull. Keep your clothes clear when the engine starts.

Emergency starting 2

There is electricity and fuel but, for whatever reason, the control box is inoperative – maybe the key is broken or lost.

WARNING

The risk of injury is very high unless the operator is very experienced and fully conversant with the normal safe operating practices of a poweboat driven by outboard engines. We are assuming that there is no safe alternative action available having taken due consideration of all the circumstances.

First separate the loom – this is the wiring plug where there are many coloured wires entering and exiting. Some looms can be found clipped in position under the hood either running parallel low down, or at an angle clipped to the side of the engine. Some engines have them outside and close to the hood. Ease the loom out of its clips and carefully separate it.

Once separated, the power circuit to the control box is now isolated. Whatever the problem at the control box it is now no longer preventing the engine from starting. The battery and power cables are still attached and linked to the starter motor. The missing ingredient is the solenoid which is activated by the key. We have bypassed this solenoid.

Go to manual starting procedure as opposite, but remove the cover (if fitted) protecting the heavy duty power cables connecting the starter motor. They are held in place by nuts and washers. (They may be protected by a rubber cover.) One of these cables is the live side and the other is the neutral. Place a large screwdriver or the tips of a pair of pliers across the end of these nuts. This takes an electrical current directly from the battery into the starter motor.

I guarantee you will jump with surprise as the starter motor flicks its cog into the flywheel, hopefully spinning the engine into life. Do not attempt this with wet hands.

When the loom is disconnected, the control box is isolated. So the key will not switch the engine off, nor will the kill cord operate. The instruments will be dead but the gears and throttle control are manually operated and, with care, you can return to base.

When back at base, remove the fuel line and allow the engine to run dry, thus stopping it.

The power circuit to the control box can be isolated on this engine by disconnecting a multi-plug, conveniently situated at the front of the engine under the hood.

Cables being used to bypass the solenoid.

Emergency starting 3

Control box inoperative and the battery flat

Go through procedure 2, then procedure 1.

WARNING
The dangers of the first two starting procedures still apply, with the added danger of the exposed flywheel.

Problem 16
Flat spots on acceleration and deceleration

As more speed is called for, the engine hesitates/falters and then pulls away. Alternatively the accelerator lever is slowly moved forward but the rpm stays the same. When the accelerator reaches a certain point, a sudden surge of power takes place. As deceleration takes place the power suddenly comes off.

Causes include:

1. A restriction of fuel. The simplest cause is running very low on fuel; alternatively there may be a restriction of fuel somewhere in the system. Remember, this can cause pre-ignition/detonation leading to operational problems and powerhead damage. (See section on detonation.)

2. Inlet jet in the carburettor sticking.

3. Spark plug breaking down.

4. Electrical timing out of sequence.

5. Worn accelerator cables sticking.

There are other possible causes of fuel restriction resulting in power loss or power surge. (See section on fuel systems.)

An easy check of the fuel to the fuel pump is to connect a separate fuel supply from a remote tank using fresh fuel.

Problem 17
Excessive smoke

Two-stroke outboards normally produce a tinge of blue exhaust smoke. This must not be confused with steam produced by the warm exhaust emitted into a cold atmosphere. The blue tinge indicates the presence of the lubricating oil.

You often get too much oil when the usual 50:1 mix has had a little more oil added just for good measure. (A 50:1 mix represents one part by volume of oil to fifty parts by volume of fuel.) Sometimes the fuel has already been pre-mixed and someone else decides to mix it again.

This excessive burning off of oil does no damage as such but could oil up the plugs and prevent the engine from running, especially at slow speeds and at idle.

Modern engines require very little oil at idle speed. Those with automatic fuel injection need as little as 200:1. At higher speeds the automatic control injects oil in greater quantities, up to the maximum of 50:1. A hand-mixed 50:1 is fine for maximum rpm, but not at very low rpm for any length of time. The oil will not burn off and will clog the spark plug/s.

Excessive oil will produce blue exhaust smoke. At best the plugs could oil up, and the slow running will become laboured. At worst, damage will be done.

Fortunately, this is an easy one to clear. Put the gear lever into neutral and select fast idle. As the rpm builds, the excessive oil will burn off in clouds of blue smoke. Please try to avoid this de-oiling exercise in marinas or upwind of other people.

However, there are other causes of excessive smoke which require more drastic attention.

They are:

1. White smoke caused by a defective head gasket or cracked head unit. (See cooling system section.)

2. Black smoke caused by the mixture being set too rich on the carburettor settings or the wrong type of spark plug, having an incorrect heat rating for the engine. (See section on spark plugs.)

3. Incorrect fuel mix or automatic oil injection supplying too much oil on demand.

If the fuel is pre-mixed, this is very easily remedied. Automatic systems require a little more thought. They can be checked by running the engine for a while at a set rpm and monitoring the oil flowing into the engine. The oil supply pipe is disconnected where it enters the engine. Oil must be pre-mixed with fuel in an external fuel tank for this test because we have diverted the oil from the engine and into a receptacle for measuring.

NOTE

It is also worth noting that modern outboard technology is making the new engines more efficient and thereby reducing fuel consumption whilst reducing the amount of two-stroke oil mix. New engines may not give any indication that oil is being burnt off

Problem 18
Troubleshooting the gearbox

The gearbox is in the lower leg and in a line with the propeller. It has no clutch mechanism and is therefore referred to as a crash gearbox. The correct selection of the gears relies on a positively smooth movement of the gear lever when the engine is at slow tickover.

The gearbox handles the engine power output, transferring its energy into the propeller. The propeller rotates in either an anticlockwise (astern) or clockwise (ahead) direction. The gear is selected by either a remote throttle and gear selection control box, or by a lever (shift handle) mounted on the side of the engine.

> **WARNING**
>   *To carry out most of the following operations the engine must be safe and unable to be started accidentally – remove the key and remove the kill cord (lanyard emergency stop switch).*

The gearbox is located at the base of the lower leg of the engine in front of the propeller and housed in a sealed unit containing its own lubricating oil. It has a filler plug (vent hole) and a draining plug. It is important that the gear oil is changed at the end of the season, especially with engines over 40 hp.

Changing the gearbox oil

First ensure the engine is as near vertical as possible and remove the vent plug at the top. As the plug is removed, turn it very slowly and listen for the air escaping from the plug as the plug washer seal is broken. If the gearbox is under pressure, as it should be, the escaping air is a very good indicator that the gearbox is in very good condition, because it immediately shows that the internal seals are still intact. (If, by

mistake, you remove the lower plug first, the oil (under pressure) will shoot out.)

Having removed the top plug remove the lower plug. The oil should be drained into a container for disposal. The colour of the oil should be slightly darker than when it went in.

Inspect the end of the lower plug. It has a magnet attached to it to collect any small particles of metal which may have been worn away during use. Any large pieces of metal, such as slivers of steel, are chipped off the teeth of the cogs. This can occur when the teeth of the cogs in the gearbox are travelling too fast at the moment of engagement. This will happen if the gear lever is taken from fast ahead to fast astern in one movement without the necessary pause in neutral to allow the cogs, engine and propeller to slow down.

Unfortunately any small pieces of metal will be stirred up in the oil and ground through the teeth of the cogs. If a large piece of metal is found, visit the engineer.

If the oil appears to be white and milky then one or more of the seals has broken down, allowing water to enter the gearbox housing. It may not be serious if it is the plug washer allowing the water to enter.

I would recommend the unit visits the engineer because the only way to check for damage is to drop the gearbox from the leg. While the lower leg is dropped it is relatively easy to check the condition of the impeller in the water pump.

Assuming that there were no chunks of metal or steel filings and very little discolouration of the oil, then the unit can be made ready for the water!

The gearbox is housed in the lower leg, which can be unbolted from the rest of the engine to service the linkage and also the water pump. It contains its own lubricating oil.

The forward and reverse linkages and drive shaft are clearly visible in this dismantled shot of a Mercury lower leg.

Use the correct marine grade of EP80 or EP90 gearbox oil as recommended by the manufacturer. This is not the same as the EP90 used on motor vehicles. (Although the grade is the same it has other additives essential for marine use.)

A dispenser is supplied with the correct oil. It has a tube which is fitted into the lower plug hole. The dispenser allows the oil to be squeezed up the tube into the base of the gearbox. Eventually the oil will appear at the top plug hole (vent).

Gearbox oil change.

1. The vent plug is unscrewed first. Note that oil is not introduced here.

4. Oil is introduced into the lower drain plug until it oozes out of the vent hole.

5. A pressurised oil dispenser makes the job much easier than relying on a gear oil tube with a fitted pipe.

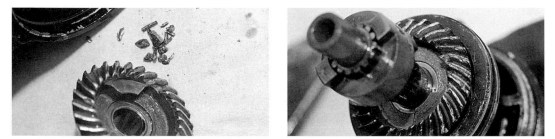

Gearbox damage can be caused by over-energetic gear changing with the revs too high; the wrong oil; no oil or penetration of water. Here the cogs have chipped off completely.

This is the only way to refill. As the oil level rises it forces the air out at the top and ensures that the gearbox has the correct quantity of oil. Apart from the hours of effort you will spend attempting to pour oil into the top hole, you cannot be sure just how much oil has gone into the gearbox rather than on the floor.

Replace the top plug while keeping pressure on the dispenser. This effectively creates a vacuum and prevents the oil from pouring out. Remove the dispenser and quickly replace the lower plug. Do not cross-thread either of the plugs: remember, it is screwing into aluminium.

2. Then the drain plug at the lowest level of the gearbox is unscrewed and the oil allowed to drain off.

3. The lower plug has a magnet to attract small pieces of metal.

6. Quickly place your finger over the drain/filler hole, and replace the top plug.

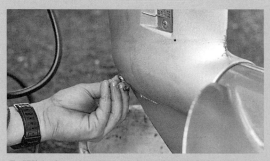

7. With the top plug replaced and tight, now is the time to insert the drain plug.

Problem 19
The engine stalls after dropping off the back of a wave

This is not a common problem but I have worked with a couple of units which occasionally stalled after I dropped the boat a couple of metres or more into a trough. The weather conditions were quite severe at the time, so it was a little worrying to have no power. Fortunately the engine re-started quickly. In both cases the equipment was set correctly and tickover was normal.

There is much debate about the best way to handle the throttle when the boat is airborne. Some say, leave it open. This puts massive strain on the engine and gearbox. Gearboxes on heavy engines have been known to fail as the propellers, travelling in excess of their design speed, are stuffed deeply into comparatively still water. The engine rpm goes way beyond its maximum. The propellers ventilate as they enter the water and – when deep down – cavitate, losing their ability to grip and thrust the boat forward. The failure occurs when the revs drop and the propellers bite.

I would recommend dropping the rpm in preparation for the moment when the propellers re-enter the water. But the instant reaction of throttling back on the controls, combined with the extra loading on the gearbox as the propellers start to grip can result in a stalled engine.

Many seconds are lost while trying to re-start without remembering to move the gear lever into neutral and many more seconds can be lost if you have knocked off the kill cord. Instantly check both gear lever position and kill cord before trying to re-start.

Pull start systems can be even more difficult because a crew member needs to move back to the engine. It is unwise to stand up in a boat in heavy seas. So often minor circumstances conspire to cause a major mishap, a clear case of one damn thing leading to another.

NOTE.
The idle speed is set with a 'normal' amount of water in the exhaust chamber. When the boat lands hard more water may be forced in, the idle rpm will not be enough to force the exhaust gases through this water and a stall results. The cure is either not to throttle back completely, or to increase the idle speed for the rough water trip

An outboard engine, as with most outdrive legs, can be adjusted with the 'up' and 'down' trim control button. The trim setting position depends upon the type of sea conditions experienced. Correct settings are only one aspect of boat control. Correct handling in a heavy sea requires very careful throttle control. Although this book is not about boat handling it is important that one hand remins on the throttle and one hand remains on the steering wheel. High speed powerboats may have a foot throttle pedal. This leaves two hands to steer. The trim buttons can be fitted to the steering wheel allowing full control of the machine. Twin engines can either be trimmed up and down together using only one button or individually to balance the boat against wind, waves and an uneven payload.

Problem 20
Troubleshooting steering controls

Most of today's engines have mild steel through-tubes on the saddle while the steering cable rod is made of stainless steel, and we all know what happens to mild steel if moisture is present – it corrodes! Units are now being manufactured of sensible material to eliminate this problem.

Gently take hold of the steering wheel and apply pressure to turn it through its full rotation in both directions. If nothing moves and you believe it to be seized please do not exert too much pressure at the steering wheel, otherwise the steering helm under the steering wheel will break and the job becomes very expensive. As soon as serious resistance is felt leave the steering wheel alone and move to the engine.

It is simple to remove the nut on the end of the steering linkage. This holds the return linkage to the fixing at the front of the engine. Spray all parts

A typical sealed wheel unit with a single cable to the steering arm.

The steering wheel contains a toothed cog into which the steering cable locks. Periodic inspection and greasing will ensure smooth turns when you most need them.

The steering helm broken down showing cog assembly.

The rack and pinion assembly.

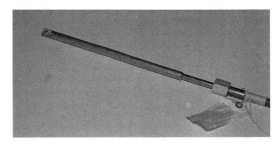

The steering rod passes through the saddle and is bolted to the steering arm attached to the engine. Corrosion will jam the rod inside the saddle unless they are maintained regularly.

Use mole grips to grip the steering rod (not the flat that takes the nut) and turn it to free it from saddle, having first sprayed liberally with freeing solution.

liberally with releasing oil.

Grip the nut in mole grips and twist slowly to free off. Do not place the grips onto the flat end from which you have just removed the nut. All you will turn is the internal cable and not the rod that is seized.

If it starts to turn you will need someone at the steering wheel to help you move the rod in and out. Gentle pressure please. Hopefully it will release instantly and move quite freely. Spray with releasing oil and clean with rag until the rod moves smoothly and emerges from the saddle tube looking clean. Replace the linkage, re-tighten the nut and pump grease through the nipple/s at the saddle. The steering wheel should move the engine smoothly through its normal turning range.

If it's seized, use a hammer with the mole grips to start a small amount of movement. The large nuts on the other side of the engine will need to be undone before the steering rod can be withdrawn. The rod will have to be worried loose. It can take three to four hours of effort for two people before it can be reconnected. If the steering cable is damaged in the process, replace it.

Not all steering cables can be withdrawn easily from the saddle bracket as there's insufficient room between the engine and the topside of the hull. The engine will need to be unbolted from the

transom and lifted – a very expensive cure, and one that for a very small amount of effort could have been avoided.

The moral is: service the unit and work the steering from side to side at least once a month if the boat is not being used. If it's stiff, clean and re-grease it.

NOTE

Stiffness of steering can be caused by a lack of grease at the swivel bracket. The manual will outline the grease nipple/s and the recommended lubricants. (See section on swivel brackets.)

Too tight a curve in the steering cable can also cause problems. Check that the cable has as gentle a curve as possible.

Cable

Modern cables are sealed where they enter the saddle bracket. Greasing the steering does not lubricate the inner cable. If the cable becomes really sticky try this simple trick. Disconnect and remove the cable from the saddle bracket. Cut the nipple off a condom and fix it over the cable, nipple end towards the steering wheel at a point where the first nut is situated. Then seal it with tape. Tie the cable to the roof of the garage or even the top of the A frame. Fill the condom with releasing fluid and this time seal the top. Leave for 24 hours and maybe top up the fluid. The fluid will seep down towards the steering helm.

By moving the steering wheel, thoroughly work the steering cable in and out. When it moves freely re-assemble the unit.

Steering wheel

The steering helm which houses the end of the steering cable is situated under the steering wheel. The steering cable enters the steering helm and locks into an enclosed toothed cog. As the wheel is turned the cable is wound in and out when the wheel is turned to the right or left.

As the cable is pulled into the steering helm it exits into a plastic tube. Push grease into this plastic tube and turn the steering wheel back and forth. This movement will take the grease into the steering helm.

If, for whatever reason, the steering helm is dismantled – maybe a replacement steering cable has been fitted – make certain it is correctly re-assembled. It's amazing how difficult it is to turn the wheel the opposite way in which one wants to travel. Even more difficult when going astern...

Saddle bracket

The saddle bracket holds the swivel part of the engine to the fixed bracket that is bolted or hand-screwed onto the transom. It supports the engine and allows the engine to swivel by using large metal-to-metal bushes. These require greasing. You may find one or two greasing nipples down the

Excess movement either up and down or side to side in the saddle indicates wear in the swivel bushes. If there is stiffness it could be seized bushes needing greasing, not necessarily a steering problem.

length of this column. When applying grease wait until the grease appears at the top and/or bottom of this column.

Checking the swivel bushes for wear

Place one hand on the lower leg and one hand near the powerhead and apply gentle pressure in and out and sideways. There should be a small amount of movement in the saddle bushing but if it is excessive have it checked by your engineer.

If the steering becomes a little stiff to turn, it may not be the steering linkage that is at fault, but could be a lack of care and attention of the saddle bushing.

NOTE
If the steering unit fails and you can't fix it, find the

Paddles lashed either side of the hood will make an effective get-you-home steering system if all else fails. But go carefully as the torque from a big engine could throw you sideways if the rig is not balanced

(compulsory) two paddles and lash one down each side of the engine hood. These will make a get-you-home tiller. Try not to tighten the rope too much or they may damage the engine cover. Then disconnect the steering cable at the engine to allow for free movement of the emergency tiller.

Do not travel too fast. If the tiller slips the engine will flick instantly over to starboard due to the torque. Maintain contact with the kill cord by extending the cord from the control panel back to the helm.

Tools and spares for a journey abroad or away from base

These are the minimum of emergency spares you should carry, based upon the assumption that the boat will be away from its base for around a month. First, however, the engine should have been serviced prior to leaving for the trip. I know of engineers who will supply a complete travel pack of spares, and the hirer pays for what is used on his/her return. If the pack is returned unopened a small charge is deducted for the service.

Spares

Two sets of spark plugs
In-line engine fuel filter
In-line fuel filter (external, if fitted)
Spare bulb and fuel line fittings
Spare propeller – tab washer and nyloc nut
or split pin and castle nut
Spacer washer if fitted
Thrust washer
Hydraulic fluid for the power trim/tilt
Gearbox oil
Sufficient quantity of two stroke oil, certified
TC-W II or III. Be guided by the
manufacturer, especially if they have
developed their own product
Fuel connector
Fuel primer bulb
Fuel pump
Hand pull starting cord
Cable ties and masking tape
Corrosion guard spray/Duck oil/WD40
Fuel stabiliser fluid/fuel treatment fluid
Spare kill cord
Spare ignition key
Battery jump leads

Right: A tool for everything and everything in its place.

Tools to carry

Propeller spanner (torque tensioner)
Block of wood
Two long-nose spanners of different sizes
Two adjustable spanners of different sizes
Selection of screwdrivers
Hammer
Quarter drive socket set
Plug spanner

NOTE
The quarter drive socket set will fit nearly everything, but is small so only a limited amount of leverage can be exerted when tightening the nuts and bolts. This is no bad thing as most bolts are made of stainless steel, and can strip the threads if screwed over-enthusiastically into an aluminium engine.

4 Propellers

The propeller delivers the thrust to push the hull through the water. The size, shape and number of blades on the propeller will have to be selected to suit the size of engine and the shape and weight of hull if the boat is to reach the design speed.

If you know the type of powerboating you intend to do, you should know the type of hull, the size of the engine and the intended top speed you are hoping to achieve. Boat manufacturers know the maximum size of engine that each of their boats will handle.

Obviously it is no easy task to make an accurate propeller selection. The engine manufacturers give the first lead when they state the maximum design revolutions per minute of their engine. This is usually across a small band, say between 4800 and 5400rpm. However, it could be several thousand rpm higher.

This indicates the speed at which the engine should be turning when running at full throttle under normal loading. The last task is to select a

propeller of suitable proportions capable of allowing the engine to reach the required rpm.

Some of the large engines fit contra-rotating propellers, where twin installations are used. The advantage is that the torque forces are balanced and the boat tracks straighter.

Pitch

Imagine a corkscrew turning and driving itself into the cork of a bottle. Each full rotation will drive it down the distance that it takes the tip of a section of the blade to complete a rotation of 360 degrees. Take the propeller and stand it on a flat surface. Walk it, by hand, through 360 degrees following the path of one blade tip and measure the distance it walks along the flat

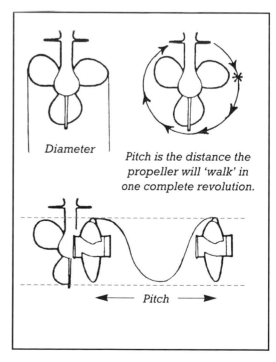

Diameter

Pitch is the distance the propeller will 'walk' in one complete revolution.

Pitch

The business end of any engine is its propeller. This one has seen better days.

This propeller spins clockwise when viewed from the stern. The stern kicks to starboard going ahead and to port in reverse, an effect known as 'prop-walk' or 'paddle-wheel effect'. It is caused by the blades having more bite in deeper water, at the bottom of their revolution, than in shallow water at the top. It can be counteracted by the trim tab or by offsetting the engine slightly to starboard. Seek advice on how much offset you need.

This propeller spins anti-clockwise when viewed from astern. The stern kicks to port going ahead.

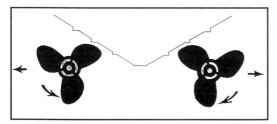

This twin-engine rig is balanced because the port engine has a counter-rotating propeller. (Unfortunately, only large outboards have the option of different handing.) Since a propeller drives more on the downstroke than the up, both are working in the cleanest water they can get – ie the efficiency is maximised.

surface in inches. That is the pitch. Inspect the propeller and you will find this information stamped on it, together with its diameter.

Theoretically one revolution of the propeller will move the boat through the water the distance of the pitch. This is not true in the real world because the blade is moving through a fluid. This fluid acts as a lubricant and permits the blade to 'slip'.

Diameter

The diameter of the propeller chosen for an outboard engine will fall within a fairly small band. Depending on the size of the engine the propeller drive shaft will be a specified distance from the anti-cavitation plate. So a propeller to fit, for example, a Mercury 75 can be selected with a slightly different diameter for the same amount of pitch, depending upon its application.

A slightly larger diameter will increase the thrust from a propeller of similar pitch. The blades will be larger and therefore have more contact with the water.

Both diameter and pitch must be taken into account when selecting the propeller

Propeller blades

A single-bladed propeller is the most efficient because the blade cuts through undisturbed water, but trying to keep a single blade in balance is impossible. Just watch an athlete trying to stay in balance when throwing the hammer – the weight tries to pull him out of the circle.

A two-bladed propeller gives better balance and yachts manage very well with two blades but they are not looking for performance, only displacement speed, and the blades are quite small.

By using three blades the performance is improved, balance is maintained and the amount of vibration is reduced. Four- and five-bladed propellers increase the area in contact with the water and can therefore have smaller diameters. Under test they have sometimes proved to be less efficient than a three-bladed propeller because of water disturbance between the blades.

Props with more blades can give a smoother delivery of power without vibration and are increasingly being used on outdrive legs.

The way one blade affects the flow of water over the next is very similar to the way the sails of a yacht interact. The disturbance of water across and through the propeller is not just caused by the blades but also by the hull.

The top of the blade when rotating in the water is travelling through this disturbed water coming off the bottom of the transom and has less grip than when the blade is cutting through less disturbed water deeper down. The blade of the propeller grips the water on the down stroke gaining maximum thrust at the bottom of its rotation. Because of torque and the greater grip lower down it tends to twist the stern. The driver could experience this effect as a tendency of the bow to turn to starboard when the engine is trimmed right down. (See section on trim tabs.)

Outboard engines usually use the centre of the hub for the escape of exhaust gases and this reduces the surface area of the blade. The pitch is increased to compensate for the smaller blade. This is ideal when we are working with high speed hulls and outboard engines.

If the pitch is increased too much the blades are unable to deliver the power and they effectively stall. Exactly the same principle applies to the way in which a sail can stall on a yacht if the angle between the sail surface and the apparent wind becomes too broad and the laminar flow breaks down.

When the flow over a propeller blade breaks down the propeller slows down, the engine rpm

is reduced and the engine is unable to reach its design speed.

So it is important that the chosen propeller meets the average requirements of the desired use of the boat, at the same time allowing the engine to perform correctly. A propeller with a large diameter and a large pitch has greater thrust than a propeller with a small diameter and small pitch. The first is ideal on a workboat and the latter ideal for a fast planing boat.

Setting up the propeller

Firstly be guided by the manufacturer's/ engineer's suggestion. Put the boat into the water with its normal load and, assuming the engine is run in, take it up to maximum speed. The tachometer reading should be at or near the maximum recommended rpm. If the engine calls for 5400 rpm maximum and it is running at 5700 rpm a propeller with an increased pitch or diameter is required.

As a general rule of thumb, a difference of 1 in of pitch can alter the engine speed by as much as 300 rpm. A propeller with a larger pitch will reduce the top rpm, whereas a lower pitch will increase the rpm.

If the outboard is being used on rivers where speed limits are in force, I would suggest a propeller with a smaller pitch to allow the engine to run happily at a higher rpm. Paint this propeller a bright colour to identify it, and change this for the correct propeller when going to the open sea and high speed.

Continual excessive revs can cause serious damage to an engine. Serious damage can also be caused when a propeller of too large a pitch is used, especially when the engine is under load.

If a performance engine is being used for towing it must be used sensibly at displacement hull speed. Open the throttle wide and the

Damage like this is easily sustained but may be repairable. A concrete slipway was the most probable cause.

The centre hole takes the shaft. The rubber bush is between the shaft and the outer rim of the propeller and it may have saved the gearbox.

engine/s will probably only reach 2/3rd maximum rpm. The fuel/air mixture, set for full rpm, will be wrong and wear will result. The smaller propeller will allow the towboat's engine to reach its designed speed.

Cavitation

Cavitation occurs when a propeller loses its grip on the water because it spins too quickly or has too much loading. The faster spin creates a 'hole' in the water (in other words a vacuum) resulting in imploding air bubbles, causing disturbance and vibration between the blades. The implosions suck particles of metal from the surface of the propeller. Continual cavitation can effectively eat away a stainless steel propeller. In the long term the vibration of the prop can move through the gearbox and into the engine.

If cavitation is a continual problem it may be wise to fit a propeller designed to handle the imploding bubbles of air. By reducing the trailing edge of the propeller the cavitation effect takes place away from the surface of the blade, thus reducing vibration and damage. These are known as cavitating propellers.

Ventilation

Cavitation is often used incorrectly to describe what is in fact ventilation. A propeller ventilates when it sucks air down from the surface of the water into the blades, creating slip. The laminar flow of the water is disturbed.

Ventilation can occur where the hull is in the fast planing mode and is put into a very tight turn, drawing surface air under the hull and into the propeller. This can easily be avoided by trimming the bow down. This increases the wetted surface area of the hull and forces the chines to cut through the water, preventing sideslip. It helps to maintain the control into the turn and finally delivers a very fast tightly-controlled turn with power applied, without sucking air into the propeller.

Air is also induced into the propeller if it is set too close to the surface of the water. So the problem can be alleviated by lowering the height of the transom. Finally, if the engine is trimmed too high the propeller may cut the surface and suck air into the blades.

Lower leg and propeller

The lower leg takes the power unit below the surface of the water. It houses the gearbox and the water pump. It is where the engine thrust is transferred through a propeller to move the boat through the water.

> **WARNING**
> **Always remove the spark plugs before working on or near a propellor.**

Each time the boat is launched and recovered carry out a visual check of the unit for damage. Please check that the skeg is intact and if any paint has been removed, exposing the aluminium, attend to it under normal maintenance.

Propeller

The propeller should be undamaged, although the edges of the blade of aluminium propellers will deteriorate with extensive use. This is usually caused by the very small particles of sand in suspension acting as a very fine abrasive, especially where the water moves quickly over shallow sandy areas and stirs up the sediment. The blades will also deteriorate rapidly if the propeller is the wrong size for the unit or has been incorrectly set up.

Extensive damage to the propeller can be caused by striking hard floating objects or by running aground. Both aluminium and stainless steel propellers can be destroyed this way. I have seen stainless blades bent and twisted through 180 degrees from running up a concrete slipway under power.

Damaged aluminium blades can be rebuilt very successfully without incurring too great an expense, provided there is sufficient material left on the blade to supply the repair specialist with a pattern and base from which to work.

Shear pin

Older style engines had a shear pin. This was fitted inside the hub of the propeller and keyed into the propeller shaft. When the propeller struck a solid object the soft metal of the shear pin snapped instantly. This disconnected the drive from the propeller preventing damage to the gearbox. A shear pin will only be found in very small outboard engines and older engines.

Checking the shear pin

With the engine running, and in the water, put the engine into forward gear on slow tickover and watch the propeller slowly spin. As acceleration is increased the propeller should

increase its revolutions pro rata. However, if the pin has snapped the propeller may even slow down or stop rotating completely. This is a sure indicator that the shear pin has snapped.

Alternatively, out of the water, put the engine into gear and gently try to rotate the propeller. If the shear pin has snapped, the propeller will spin on its shaft with very little resistance.

WARNING
Remove spark plugs before working near the propellor to ensure the engine cannot start up. If the engine starts by turning the propeller , a fatal accident could happen.

Replacing the shear pin

Remove the split pin from the locking nut on the end of the propeller shaft and undo the nut. Gently remove the propeller and cup your hand underneath to catch the three pieces of the shear pin. Replace with a new shear pin and reassemble the unit, finishing with a replacement split pin.

If you have no spare shear pin aboard it may just be possible to re-arrange the three pieces of the old one in a different order. They do not always break in three even lengths. By replacing the pieces differently, a broken end may just locate into the shaft with sufficient length of metal to lock the propeller for a slow run home.

In an emergency a cut-down nail may be used but be careful: it will not snap on impacting the propeller with a solid object.

Rubber bushes

Propellers now have rubber bushes inside, bonded with the spline and held in place inside the hub by pressure. The bush will then slip on the spline when a blade hits a solid object.

Checking the bush

After an immense amount of use, water can

The propeller should come off easily; if not the splines will need greasing. Note the water cooling intake grill which can become encrusted with marine life if the leg is neglected and left immersed.

This propeller uses the common split pin and castle nut method. The peripheral holes in the hub let out the exhaust. Older engines may have a shear pin, of which spares should be carried.

sometimes get between the rubber bush and the inside surface of the propeller hub. This acts as a lubricant and it is possible for the propeller to slip when accelerating hard, thereby reducing the power output. There are two ways of checking: first when the boat is on full power and under load in the water, and second by using a tension bar when the engine is out of the water.

One of my propellers started to fail after 2000 hours of use. It is not cost effective to replace the bush on a small propeller. It is more economical to start afresh with a new unit. This may not be the answer for expensive propellers.

Changing the propeller

There are three methods used to prevent the propeller falling off: a castle nut locked in place by either a cotter pin/split pin, a Nyloc nut, or a standard type of locking nut held in place by a tab washer.

Castle nut

1. Remove the pin and undo. Remove the castle nut by placing a block of wood between the propeller blade and the anti-cavitation plate for leverage.

2. Remove the spacer washer.

1. This propeller is held on by a nut and tab washer. A block of wood is used to stop the propeller turning while the nut is freed.

2. The tab washer is removed and the propeller pulled or gently tapped off the splines.

3. Remove the propeller – it should tap off gently using a block of wood.

4. Sitting on the propeller shaft behind the propeller is the thrust bushing or thrust washer (this may be incorporated in the back of the propeller). Remove this bush.

5. Clean and apply the correct grease to the length of the shaft.

6. Re-assemble the propeller but do ensure the thrust bushing is in place correctly and likewise that the propeller seats onto this bush. Failure to replace the thrust bush will result in the propeller driving itself into the gearbox, causing total destruction of the gearbox and housing.

7. Finally install the spacer and tighten the castle nut. Replace the cotter pin and spread the ends to lock the castle nut. It may be a good idea to place a propeller lock on the end of the shaft.

Nyloc nut

1. Bend the tab washer away from the nut.

2. Place a block of wood between the propeller and the anti-cavitation plate as above.

3. Undo the nut with a propeller spanner – then

continue as above but using the Nyloc nut and tab washer.

All the necessary tools and components, including a replacement cotter pin/tab washer, should be carried aboard in case you need to remove and replace a damaged propeller at sea. Tie a large plastic bin liner over the lower leg so you have sufficient room to work inside: any tool or component dropped will fall into the bin liner rather than to the bottom of the sea.

An alternative technique is to bring another well-fendered boat alongside and work from it. Or a crew member, dressed appropriately, and attached to the boat, can sort out the problem – but any engines close by must be switched off. (Having the engine out of gear and on tickover is too dangerous.)

WARNING

Please remove all spark plugs. Never enter the water from a powerboat unless it is essential for the safety of crew and boat. Never allow a person to go overboard into the water unless it is possible for that person to be returned aboard safely.

3. In most engines the thrust washer (or thrust bushing) looks like this. Regrease them before replacing the propeller, washer and nut.

4. Finally the tab washer is bent back to lock the nut in place.

5 Hydraulic & Manual Trim & Tilt

These hydraulic units are from a Mercury 75. The rams, motor cabling, filler plug and bleed screw are all visible.

All outboards are easy to install and remove from boats if you have the correct equipment. Once fitted, they need to be lifted in and out of the water, either manually or hydraulically. Small engines can be lifted and carried around fairly easily. Larger units of 20 hp and over become too heavy to move easily and very large ones will need a crane. Once seated on the transom they pivot with a proportion of their weight on either side and therefore become much more manageable.

There are two types of tilt mechanism: manual and automatic. The manual method relies on locking levers and pins, whereas the automatic system is battery driven and operated by either a button or a rocker switch at the helm. Some engines have an extra rocker button on the outside (the trailer button). Both mechanisms have their advantages and disadvantages.

Manual trim and tilt

This method is preferable with smaller engines up to, say, 40 hp and particularly those on small rescue craft used by sailing schools and clubs. The engine can be lifted very quickly which is important when approaching a lee shore fast. If the boat is to be used in water noted for driftwood and flotsam, the manual lift is much more suitable (and reduces the initial cost of the engine). The locking down lever can be disconnected and the engine will flip out of the water on impact and drop back down.

A certain amount of strength and expertise is required to tilt larger engines manually. Also the crew member operating the levers is positioned at the stern of the boat where he is at risk of becoming injured or falling overboard.

Automatic trim and tilt

Hydraulic trim and tilt is recommended for large engines and on engines fitted to craft operating in more controlled conditions. It is excellent when working in shallow water and has the added benefit of finer adjustment for correctly setting the angle of the propeller. This is vital for the correct balance of the boat and is found only by trial and error. It is determined by the shape and style of the hull, the speed of travel, the all-up weight – including fuel and crew – and the wave conditions. With manual tilt, only a general setting can be found.

The trim and tilt hydraulic power system incorporates an electric motor and a fluid-filled pressurised reservoir, a pump, trim cylinder and a tilt ram. In some cases, trim rods are included. All of these components are located next to the lower leg assembly under the engine.

How it works

To lower the engine, press the down button/rocker switch, which is usually located on the end of the gearshift control lever. Electricity flows to the solenoid which passes electricity to the motor which pumps fluid under pressure through the valves on the downside. This pressure forces the ram downwards, the ram is attached to the engine and the engine is thus lowered. The reverse happens when the engine is lifted.

As soon as the switch or rocker button is released, the pump stops and the engine will remain locked in situ. The fluid will remain locked and under equal pressure both sides of the valves.

Far greater pressure is required to lift than to lower the engine, particularly when using the trim control at speed. The up side pressure will be at least 1300 psi whereas the down side operates on gravity and/or propeller thrust and can be around 500 psi. The down side is also required to hold the engine down when engaging reverse gear. The low maximum pressure to keep the engine down helps to protect the engine if the boat is run aground. On severe impact the engine will override the pressure, allowing the engine to tilt up. Override valves, known as relief valves or check valves, prevent the system from exploding on impact, or if the switch is left in the on position when the engine has reached its stops.

Damage may still occur if the boat is travelling too fast on impact for the relief valves to operate, or is travelling through soft mud, sand or shingle when the lower leg may impact with insufficient energy to release the pressure.

Several sorts of damage can result:

1. The engine can be wrenched off at the transom.

2. The lower leg can be sliced off, destroying the gearbox.

3. When the engine remains down in the mud, etc, the propeller, water pump, gearbox housing and gears are at risk by being dragged along the seabed.

Hydraulic systems are, on the whole, very reliable and basically maintenance free if used and serviced regularly. However, some other problems may be encountered, such as:

1. A low battery giving insufficient power to drive the motor, or no power at all to operate the motor (the engine can be up or down).

The Mercury's bleed screw will allow the leg to drop down when released. Note the twin hydraulic rams.

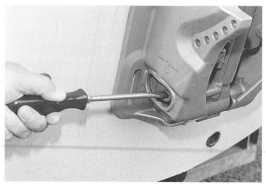

The Honda's bleed screw is opened to override the electrically-operated valves. (This photo also shows the trim adjustment pin holes.)

2. The boat overturned with the engine in the down position, preventing a recovery.

3. An electrical fault. As with any pressurised hydraulic system, there must be an override, rather like a hydraulic car jack. By controlling the amount of fluid released, the car can be lowered gently.

With trim and tilt, the lifting and lowering is controlled by an electric motor. If there is a problem, the outboard can be lifted or lowered manually. It is a very much more sophisticated unit than the hydraulic car jack but the principles bear some resemblance.

Manual override

From the service manual, find the manual release valve. Using the recommended tool, turn the screw or plug three or four turns anti-clockwise. Take hold of the lower leg and lift gently. The engine should lift fully until you can engage the tilt lock lever. When locked, retighten the screw. If the manual release valve screw/plug is accidentally removed, all fluid will be lost. (See section on filling and bleeding.)

If the engine is stuck up, but needs to be down, first ensure that it can be lowered safely. Then undo the manual release valve and gravity will lower the engine. Finally, retighten the release valve. (Support the engine while

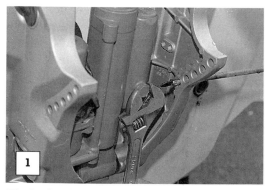

The hydraulic filler nut on a Honda.

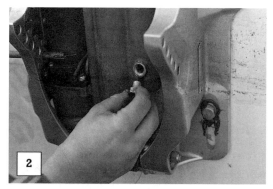

Use the tilt lock lever to keep the engine up when undoing the nut to prevent fluid being forced out.

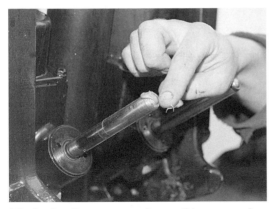

The hydraulic rams are given a thin smear of anti-corrosion greases.

undoing the release valve. If you don't it will fall fast and may hurt anyone who is in the way.)

If an engine has been left for several months in the tilted position and refuses to trim down, it is possible that the fluid has seeped past the valves.

Assuming all other functions are correct, follow the course of action given above, and, after securing the manual relief value, it should work.

Filling and bleeding

The hydraulic system may need to be topped up if:

3

Filling the hydraulic ram. Fill until a dribble appears.

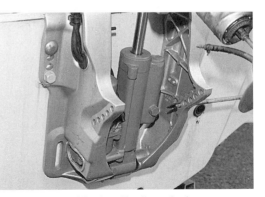

The saddle and hydraulic tilt and trim on a Honda. Note the drop-nose pin to the left which limits the ultimate movement of the leg, a feature on both manual and automatic tilt and trim engines.

1. The engine trims down, but will not trim up under load.

2. The tilt and trim works with a very slow or jerky movement.

Possible causes may be a leaking component, or air in the system. As with all pressurised hydraulic units, there must be a way of filling and bleeding the system.

First, check the service manual and identify the fill screw at the top of the reservoir. Set the engine in the tilted up position, as high as it will go. Lock it by using the tilt lock lever. It must be in this position otherwise the hydraulic fluid will squirt out when the fill screw is removed. Slowly remove the fill screw, then check the level of fluid. It should be visible. If necessary, top up with the automatic transmission fluid recommended by the manufacturer. If you are unsure as to the correct procedure, speak to the engineer.

Cleaning and greasing

Units fitted with trim rods can make horrible metallic creaking noises. On some models there is a roller bearing in a cup on top of the rod. It's there to prevent friction between the end of the rod and the metal of the engine saddle. If left unattended it will corrode and jam. The pressure and grinding action may also damage the rods. Clean and lube the roller bearing with the approved anti-corrosion grease. The trim will now operate without creaking.

Trim adjustment pin

This pin is situated at the lowest part of the saddle and restricts the engine from pivoting down too low. It prevents the boat travelling nose down at speed and becoming unstable. This pin can only be placed correctly by testing a fully loaded boat in the water and is a feature on both automatic and manual tilting.

Depending on the construction and use of the engine and the boat, some models may be set up without this adjustment pin in place.

Trim and indicator gauge

The trim gauge, mounted on the console, relays the engine position, although it's wise to check visually before starting. It can be a useful aid if the engine is out of sight of the driver, but the indicator is not sensitive enough to be relied on for the final adjustment.

NOTE
The trim position will vary each time the boat is used. The correct setting depends on the weight and position of the fuel and crew, plus the wave formation and direction of travel.

Sacrificial anode

The lower part of the trim and tilt mechanism is usually partially immersed in the water and therefore subject to electrolysis (galvanic corrosion). To avoid corrosion and damage, an anode is attached at the lowest point of the unit. Replace this anode when about half of it has been consumed. It shouldn't be painted or protected.

6 Sacrificial Anodes & Electrolysis

Electrolysis – or the decomposition of a substance by the application of an electric current – is an outboard killer. The sacrificial anode is designed to be eaten away and acts as a decoy to prevent a similar process occurring on your expensive engine casing.

The process is simple. Any metal connected to an electrical power supply and left immersed in salt water will act in a similar way to the anodes in a battery. An outboard is mainly aluminium, sits in salt water and is often permanently connected to a battery. The metal will eventually erode away.

Anodes are attached to parts of the engine which are immersed in the water. The different sections of the engine can be wired up to ensure that the unit makes a complete circuit and the zinc is attacked before the painted aluminium.

I know of a boat which was swamped and sank on its mooring. It was on the bottom for 24 hours. The sealed battery kept up the supply of electrical current and when the boat was lifted and the engine inspected, the bank of carburettors had disappeared, leaving only the nuts and bolts in situ. Manufacturers normally site a large anode under the saddle.

Trim tabs

The trim tab under the anti-cavitation plate acts as another anode (see section on trim tabs) and another smaller inset anode can be fitted above the plate.

Checking the anodes

Visually check the anodes and if they are heavily pitted and/or have sections missing and/or have become very powdery then replace them. The anode under the saddle will require replacement when 50 per cent has been eroded.

The sacrificial anode on this Honda has plenty of meat left, but will need replacing eventually.

The next line of attack after this trim tab anode goes will be the engine.

This horror story involved one perfectly serviceable outboard which was left immersed in salt water too long without cathodic protection. The gearbox dropped off.

NOTE

The zinc anodes will not always protect the engine. When fresh water is contaminated by minerals and has certain oxidising properties, the lower unit can be corroded away leaving the anode intact. In this case the engine will need to be removed completely from the water.

I have seen serious corrosion to outboard engines which have been left on moorings in a small fresh water lake which has a certain type of deposit in the water. They were new engines, completely protected by paint and had anodes, yet the painted surface of the lower leg was spotted and deeply pitted by erosion leaving the anode intact. If they had been left for a few more months, the gearbox would have fallen away.

Electrolysis

Erosion of the engine will take place if:

1. The paint on the lower leg is heavily scored or removed by driving the outboard through sand and shingle. This can expose too much aluminium for the anodes to protect, so prime and repaint using recommended paints.

2. Incorrect greases have been used. For example, grease containing graphite will form a galvanic cell (producing an electric current by chemical action). Please only use recommended lubricants.

3. The zinc anodes have been painted! Never paint anodes. If painted they will have to be replaced.

4. The outboard has been tilted so far out of the water that the anodes have been lifted clear – yet part of the engine bracket remains in the water – or the tip of the skeg just breaks the surface. Ensure the circuit connecting the anodes is not broken, and/or install an extra zinc anode below the waterline.

Alternatively, leave the engine down, but not if the boat is going to dry out on its mooring. This could have a further knock-on effect of weed and crustaceans building up in the water intake.

5. The boat was removed from the sea and the engine was not flushed through with fresh water and/or the outside of the engine was not washed down with fresh water. Salt crystals will remain inside and outside the aluminium body of the engine. With very high humidity, the moisture in the atmosphere will adhere to the salt crystals. A cell will form and electrolysis will take place.

6. A stainless steel propeller shaft may also erode when a fishing line or other form of material becomes tightly wound around it, preventing oxygen from reaching its surface. This can cause crevice corrosion – it is therefore important that the propeller shaft is checked and any material wrapped around it is removed.

7. When the boat is moored above an iron deposit such as a heavy anchor or mooring chains the reaction can be alarming. I have

Some engines have this extra anode fitted under the anti-cavitation plate.

returned after about an hour to find effervescence around the lower legs of the outboard. This is similar to the bubbles seen rising to the surface of a wet battery on trickle charge. The anodes were doing their job but for how long could they last against such an attack? We moved the boat!

An engine removed from the sea and left without attention for month after month can literally drop off the back of the boat. Very few engines wear out – they erode away quietly in someone's back yard.

Painting aluminium

Avoid cleaning the body of the engine with a wire brush. Small particles of steel can become trapped within the aluminium surface and cause galvanic cells. Use a nylon or bristle brush.

Do use a recommended base primer and finish with the manufacturer's recommended topcoat. Treat any blistering or corrosion of the bodywork immediately.

7 Winterisation & Service

Few engines are used over the winter period, but it is foolhardy to neglect them during this time. How can they be expected to start at the beginning of the season when they have been left under a damp tarpaulin for several months? You wouldn't expect a car to fare any better if left in a similar situation.

DIY winterisation, without the services of an engineer, is possible and if carried through correctly should avoid many of the following problems. What follows is a quick and simple method of preparing an engine for storage even during the worst weather.

A quick squirt of corrosion inhibitor is hardly enough to protect an expensive engine over a harsh winter. For trouble-free running next season follow a strict regime.

Step One

Prepare the engine for normal running in a large dustbin-sized tank of water. Do not use the flushing device because the cold water will prevent the engine from reaching the correct running temperature and the thermostat will fail to open.

Flushing out the engine with fresh water after every session will mean less trouble at season's end. Salt water is an engine's worst enemy. Note the large anti-cavitation plate fitted to improve propeller 'bite'.

To gain access to the air intake on the carburettor, remove the air filters. Carry out the normal checks and ensure the water is turned on at the hose tap before starting. Run the engine and check the tell-tale is strong. Run for about five minutes on fast tickover, or until

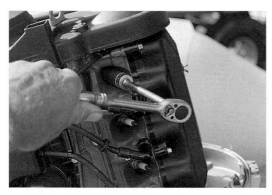

Proper tools are essential and make even the simplest jobs, like taking out the plugs, much easier.

Remove the propeller. Clean the splines then grease them before putting the propeller back on. Alternatively the shaft can be greased and wrapped in a plastic bag (minus prop) for the winter.

warm. Remove the fuel line without switching the engine off.

The engine will continue to run for several minutes, using the fuel in the carburettors. Now is the time to inhibit the engine. Begin spraying 'storage seal' into the air intakes of the carburettors, alternating between them to ensure each receives a good quantity of the sealant. Eventually, the engine will stop. Switch off the ignition. To ensure the carburettors are dry of fuel, remove the drain plugs on each one. When completely dry, re-tighten the drain plug screws.

The spraying of storage seal into the air intakes is probably sufficient to protect the internal moving parts of the engine over a winter period. However, if storing for a particularly long time or in very damp conditions, it is recommended you carry out Step Two.

Step Two

Remove the spark plugs and pour a small quantity of two-stroke oil into each plug hole. Replace the plugs and turn the engine over, either by hand or by using the starter motor (with the kill cord off), making absolutely certain that she cannot fire up accidentally. This second

stage doubles the oiling of the pistons and prevents the piston rings from seizing up. (At the beginning of the following season, there will be plenty of lubrication oil to permit the free movement of the piston without causing score marks in the cylinder.)

Replace the air filters, but before replacing the hood spray the engine with a liberal amount of the recommended corrosion guard, or a mixture of light oil and paraffin (duck oil). This is not a penetrating oil and does not set into a hard skin.

Avoid water displacement fluid because the film left behind sets and can conduct electricity and cause tracking on the high tension leads.

Grease all linkages with a recommended marine grease. Some engines have nylon/fibre moving parts and therefore do not require grease. If unsure whether to grease or not, it is better to be safe than sorry and grease all moving parts. Grease on nylon/fibre units will not be harmful and may protect them from the intrusion of dirt. Do not use car greases because they are not compatible with salt water and marine components.

The saddle is greased via nipples. A steering rod seized in the saddle bracket will spoil your first balmy days of spring and a few judicious dabs of grease now will work wonders.

Propeller

Remove the propeller and clean the spline. Use the correct grease, usually coloured green, and then replace the propeller. Alternatively, cover the spline with grease and then a plastic bag and put the propeller and fittings away until required. Take care not to misplace the thrust washer. (See section on propellers.)

Engine bodywork

Thoroughly wash the outside casing and hood of the engine with warm water and car shampoo. Dry off and polish, as you would a car.

Steering controls

If you use the manufacturer's recommended anti-corrosion grease (which will not go sticky and hard) the steering unit should move freely, particularly if you can move it a few times during the layup. (Refer to the section on troubleshooting steering.)

Battery

Before removing the battery, trim the engine down into the vertical position for storage and try and keep it in a dry well-ventilated area.

The batteries used are often referred to as 'maintenance free' but if you're storing an engine over a winter period the battery should be removed from the boat and kept in a cool dark place. Do not place batteries directly onto concrete as they tend to sweat.

If the solution is low top up with distilled water to a level somewhere between the 'min' and 'max' indicators. During the winter it is wise to trickle charge monthly and the battery will then be ready for the new season.

When working around batteries do follow the handling instructions regarding acid. If your clothing becomes contaminated, immediately wash down with copious quantities of fresh water. Do the same if your skin or eyes come into contact with the acid and also seek immediate medical attention.

Start of season

If the winterisation was carried out correctly the preparation for the new season will be minimal.

Clouds of white smoke will probably be evident after first starting up for the new season as excess oil is burnt off.

This Honda has engine as well as gearbox oil which will need replacing periodically.....

... and the filter will need changing at the same time, remembering to smear a little fresh oil on the seal before fitting hand tight.

1. Remove the battery from storage and ensure that it is fully charged.

2. If the engine was stored without the propeller, fit it correctly as described earlier.

3. Thoroughly clean or replace the spark plugs. The first start up might prove difficult because of the large quantity of oil in the cylinders from winterisation.

4. Check the level of the oil in the gearbox and, if necessary, top up.

5. Lubricate and grease all nipples and linkages – refer to the manual.

6. Completely clean the engine and polish the painted surface.

7. If the engine is fitted with automatic oil injection it would be wise to check that there is no air in the system. Slacken the air bleed screw and check that oil is flowing without any signs of air. If the engine is operated without oil it will be seriously damaged.

8. Increase the quantity of oil in the oil/petrol mix for the first few minutes of operation.

9. Attach the muffs and the hosepipe for water circulation, and turn on the tap.

10. Hand pull the engine or spin on the starter motor with the kill cord off. This ensures the free movement of moving parts.

11. Ensure that fresh fuel is primed into the carburettors.

12. Start up using the normal procedure for cold starting.

13. When the engine starts there will be clouds of white smoke as the excess oil is burnt off. When it starts to run smoothly (and after it has warmed up to the normal temperature) switch off and put in a new set of spark plugs. (Do not run at excessively high rpm.)

14. Check the steering controls.

8 Fuel

Fuel tanks are made of several different materials, generally mild steel but also plastic and glassfibre. In-built tanks are often made out of stainless steel, which can be custom made to fit under the console or built into the hull.

The tanks aboard rescue boats are placed as low down as possible for maximum stability. Fuel can also be stored in flexible tanks that take up the shape of the space between hull and deck, thereby containing the greatest volume of fuel.

Some tanks will be integral with the hull structure, bonded, treated and sealed during building.

Portable tanks

The common 5.5 gallon (25 litre) steel tank should be checked inside for rust and/or water and debris. The mild steel bottom will rust after a time, leaving rust marks on the floor of the boat.

All remote fuel tanks need to be secured, ideally with straps having quick release buckles, to stop them breaking loose and causing damage.

Water in the fuel is serious and will affect the running of the engine. The water can be removed or dispersed, but the tank may have to be replaced if it shows considerable signs of corrosion.

If left unattended the filler cap on the metal tank can become a problem. A common type has a vacuum release valve which screws down tightly to prevent spillage. The valve needs to be unscrewed to allow the fuel pump on the engine to draw out a steady and sufficient quantity of fuel from the tank. The valve is usually mild steel and must be greased regularly, or it will seize in the closed position and the tank won't vent. Try turning the cap and valve by hand. If it will only turn by using a pair

Good fuel cleanliness starts at the tank. This rigid steel tank has a male/female fuel line connector to make it easier to carry the tank ashore for filling.

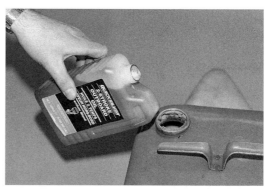

Pour the correct amount of oil in first, then top up with fuel and shake the can to mix.

of pliers, it won't be long before it snaps off.

Make an external check of the lower rim and handles and rim of the cap. If any signs of rust are present, drain the tank of petrol and leave to dry. Then with a wire brush remove any loose metal back to the metal surface of the tank, ensuring that the rust dust does not enter the tank. Paint the tank with a zinc-based primer, followed by a top coat of good quality paint. Pay special attention to the base of the tank.

Storing fuel over the winter

There are two schools of thought: either completely fill the tanks for winter, or completely drain them. The first method eliminates internal corrosion on the inside of tank, but the condition of the fuel at the beginning of the next season will be suspect. Fuel has a shelf life and will become stale after a short while. (See section on fuel.)

The second procedure entails draining off the fuel and drying the tank before treating it for any corrosion. Place the tank upside down while in storage as this will also eliminate the risk of corrosion. At the beginning of the new season fill with newly purchased fuel.

Having completed any repairs necessary, spray with a light oil or duck oil.

Security

A 25-litre tank of fuel is very heavy, so do check the strops for wear and ensure that they can be tightened and will stay tight.

Fuel fittings

Make regular checks of fuel pipes and connections for wear because the rubber tube can become cracked and split. The internal seating of one type of connector has been known to disintegrate, letting fuel spill and air enter the system. It is easier to draw air than petrol through a tube, therefore any break in

A funnel like this will usually have a mesh filter to augment the one in the tank itself. Keep funnels and tanks spotless, watching out for rust.

the fuel line will result in the engine fuel pump sucking a mixture of air and fuel.

Avoid sitting on the fuel tank or treading on the fuel pipe or its fittings. I recall one such case where the connector had been snapped off and the helmsman had stuck it back on by wrapping it with Sellotape. However, petrol attacks Sellotape and after ten minutes it all fell apart and he was forced to paddle back to base.

Gasoline (petrol)

The quality of the fuel is of paramount importance to users of outboard engines. The majority of outboard engine breakdowns are attributed to a fuel problem, the most

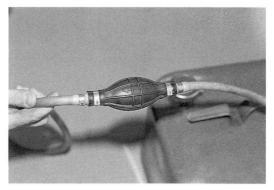

The rubber priming valve has a long life but will crack eventually. It has a built-in non-return valve.

When purchasing fuel it is important to:

1. Obtain it from a large major retailer who has a fast turnover of stock.

2. Purchase it as and when required.

3. Avoid storage over the winter. But if there is no alternative, fuel treatment additives can be added.

4. When running the engine up on the muffs at the end of the day, detach the fuel line and allow the engine to run out of fuel. This will virtually guarantee that the next time the engine is used it will start first time.

5. Add the recommended fuel conditioner when required.

---

embarrassing of all being the boat running out of petrol!

Petrol is produced to satisfy a whole different range of engines and has not been specifically designed for outboard engines. Technical words such as octane, volatility, oxidation stability, detergency, Research Octane Number (RON) and Motor Octane Number (MON) describe different features of petrol.

In the UK the different properties are controlled by the British Standard Institution (BSI) 4040 and 7070. The USA uses a different system to measure the octane rating in fuel and arrives at a lower figure than the equivalent figure for fuels used in Europe. In Europe RON is used, which is based on research of an engine operation at 'moderate speed' and in 'mild operation'. This figure is the octane rating on the petrol pumps in Europe.

In the USA, MON is used. This is measured at a 'very high speed' with a 'high loading' and in a mode of 'severe operation'. The resultant octane figure will be much lower than the European figure. The testing and measuring of the fuel quality is so different in the USA that an octane rating of 87 converts to a European RON of 92.

When the American figure is converted to the equivalent UK octane rating, a minimum figure of 92 is reached. Unleaded petrol in the UK has an octane rating of a minimum of 95 and leaded petrol of 97 (minimum).

Unleaded fuel was first available in the USA in the 1970s and today leaded petrol is no longer used. It therefore follows that all American outboard engines (and sterndrives) are designed to run on (USA) unleaded petrol.

Octane

Octane rating is the ability of the petrol to burn normally within certain conditions. The manufacturer's chosen fuel for your engine will allow your engine to run at the correct temperature and speed. However, when the octane is too low, or where the fuel mixture through the carburettor is too weak (poor carburettor settings), or where the ignition timing is set too far advanced (poor ignition timing settings) a common form of abnormal combustion is experienced called 'knock', 'pinking' or 'detonation'. This is a spontaneous combustion of the fuel and air mixture.

This takes place in the cylinder at the wrong time (before the spark) and is similar to a hammer blow on top of the piston. The objective

Who knows what lurks inside the engine. This cylinder shows signs of severe abuse, which even a non-expert would discover if he asked for a test run.

behind proper ignition is to force the piston in the direction of the down stroke. But pre-ignition strikes the piston before or at the top of its stroke.

Another symptom of low octane is that the engine continues to run after it has been switched off. The long term result of running with low octane fuel and/or incorrect engine settings is damage to the cylinder, piston and piston rings with heavy carbon deposits and fraying cylinder head gaskets (if fitted). Engine 'knock' can break down the big end bearings. The importance of correct fuel cannot be over-stressed.

Volatility

This expresses the speed with which the fuel will vaporise and is governed by temperature and pressure. Fuel used in the summer months has been prepared with a different volatility

from the fuels used in the winter months.

A fuel with a high volatility can vaporise on its route to the engine in either the lines, carburettor or where it becomes close to a very hot component. In the winter high volatility will help with cold starting. Summer will see a reduction in volatility and fuel bought then may prove difficult if used for starting an engine in the winter.

Fuel that is too volatile can cause loss of power, stalling and difficulty in re-starting when the engine is hot. Volatility is therefore a compromise by the fuel companies depending on the time of the year. Purchase your fuel as and when you need to use it.

Oxidation

Petrol will oxidise in the presence of air and the amount of oxidation depends on several factors.

Petrol left for a long time in a static form will evaporate and form gums which can block the carburettor jets.

Try to avoid leaving full fuel tanks static over long periods because the fuel will become stale with a drop in octane. Be careful when fuel is purchased from waterside petrol pumps where the turnover of stock may be limited and the storage conditions may not be ideal.

If globules of water can be seen resting on the bottom of the tank, take immediate action. Water in fuel is death to an outboard: when it reaches the carburettors it will block the jets. After adding the correct quantity of recommended additive leave the tank for around half an hour and on the next inspection the globules of water should have disappeared. Of course the water is still present but now broken down into small manageable particles, presenting no problem for the jets.

Many people suggest that the engine requires servicing after 20, 50 or 100 hours of use. The grease gun and the corrosion guard spray take care of most of the day-to-day running of the engine, while small items of maintenance can be dealt with as they occur. Understanding and adhering to the above should result in engine maintenance being kept to an absolute minimum. The engine could run for around 700 hours between servicing by an engineer.

Weather

An engine is usually tuned in the spring or winter when the air is cold and (probably) dry. Although correct for the winter, the propeller may need to be changed for the summer months, especially if the summer is exceptionally hot and humid.

In summer conditions when the temperature and humidity are high and the atmospheric pressure is low, the engine will be unable to reach its design performance figures. Because the power output is down, the rpm will be lower than intended unless a propeller with a smaller pitch is used. By changing the size of the propeller the engine will return to its peak performance. UK weather is unlikely to cause very much difference and it may only become critical if you are interested in high performance.

A point of interest: different places in the world have different probems. In the Caribbean any fuel pre-mixed with two-stroke oil is dead after three weeks and is thrown away. It is normal to run with a 'dry fuel' additive (10% alcohol), but even this cannot compete with the heat and humidity.

9 Swamping Leading to a Complete Dunking

Swamping in salt water

Rigid inflatable boats (RIBs) are often used in heavy weather in preference to the conventional hard hull. The RIB, with its excellent buoyancy, can be put under or through a wave and come out the other side. The water onboard is quickly drawn out of the hull through the transom flaps.

The majority of outboard engines are designed to operate in some of the most severe conditions imaginable. The hoods and air intakes are specifically designed to keep the water away from the air intakes of the carburettors. Any water entering the top of the hood air intake is diverted by gravity down the sides of the engine and out through the drain holes at the base where the engine is fixed to the top of the shaft.

I have buried engines completely under a wave for a short time and yet each time they have returned to the surface working normally. Continual and very quick dunking will not give sufficient time for the water inside to exit the drain holes. Although there is a considerable amount of air inside the hood, several dunkings in quick succession will result in flooding the hood. The water will enter the carburettors and the engine will stop. Only if the driver responds quickly enough, and quickly switches off, can he save the engine from serious damage.

Stage one

1. Remove the engine hood and allow water to drain off the engine.

2. Remove the spark plugs.

3. Drain the carburettors by undoing the drain plugs at the base of each one.

4. Pump fresh fuel through the carburettors forcing out any water. When only the fuel pours out, close the drain plugs. (Beware that the fuel may be contaminated by water.)

5. With the spark plugs removed and the kill cord off, turn the engine over. Make certain any water inside the cylinders is forced out of the open spark plug holes. A dry cloth or paper kitchen roll held over the holes will catch any moisture being forced out. (Keep a dry cloth in your waterproof container.)

6. Check that there is a spark. Then dry and replace the spark plugs, or insert replacement plugs.

7. Re-start the engine. If it fails to start after a short time, repeat the above procedure as necessary.

When back at the home base carry out the procedure for winterisation and run up in a tank (not on the muffs) for a very long time, or put the engine back in the water and run it for a long time under load.

Stage two

If, having tried the first stage, the engine fails to start, take it straight to an engineer. If this is impracticable, you will have to remove the unit from the transom and submerse it in fresh water. It will need to be left in this state until it can be stripped down.

It will probably require a full service with possibly all of the electrical parts being replaced – solenoids, switch box, charging regulators etc.

Complete immersion

This will entail everything in stage two and also attending to the battery, fuel tanks and lines, plus a strip down of the control box with the possible replacement of all electrical gauges and indicators.

If you use your boat for, say, rescue in heavy weather, when there is a risk of a complete immersion or capsize, then the engine and electrics will require complete waterproofing together with an automatic inversion bag mounted on the metal anti-roll bar at the transom ('A' frame). In this case I suggest you seek advice from the RNLI who regularly prepare their craft for such eventualities. There are also several companies specialising in the preparation of engines for involuntary immersion.

10 Secondhand Engines

A quick pull will tell you very little about an engine's state. Better a trial run to check gears and cooling.

The secondhand market offers an excellent range of boats at a reasonable price. Second-hand boats, purchased through a recognised dealer, should carry a warranty and most reputable dealers will only handle reliable packages.

Boats sold privately can be on the market for a variety of very genuine reasons. The majority of the sales I have dealt with have come about because of a change of circumstance at work or within the family and where priorities have changed. Sadly a few of the sales are because the owner has died or become too old or unwell.

A genuine reason for sale often means a genuinely good secondhand bargain. Here are a few others:

1. Because people have purchased inappropriate boats on the spur of the moment without thinking why or what they want them for.

2. On reflection and first use they discover they don't like it.

3. Maybe they had been ill-advised into a purchase. There are excellent ex-demonstration boats for sale at discounted prices and if one is not concerned about

The author getting down to it.

having the latest colour, this could prove to be a good starting point.

I well remember the disappointment of one client who found that he was too large to fit into the driving seat of his boat and therefore had to remain very much in the passive role as a crew member, until he could find a larger boat.

What to look for

I would not think of purchasing a secondhand boat unless I could see it in the water and be in a position to watch the way in which the engine and boat had been prepared for the sea. The boat does need to be driven. Starting the engine in a back yard only proves that the engine either works or doesn't work. One boat purchased after a demonstration in the back garden proved to be a very costly mistake. The gearbox was a mish-mash of broken pieces.

If you know absolutely nothing about boats then you should find someone who does, and take him with you, but beware the person who says he knows everything but in fact knows nothing.

If you do know what you're doing, ask to drive the boat. Check the amount of play in the steering. Is it very hard to turn? Does it turn through its full turning arc? Follow through the section in this book on how a healthy engine should sound and respond.

With the boat out of the water, check:

1. General overall condition of the engine. It should be clean and tidy without excessive damage. It will of course have received scuff marks and show general wear and tear.

2. The condition of the propeller and skeg.

Anodes should be in place. I would be more wary of a replacement propeller, or a freshly painted one than a propeller that showed some sign of use. If it has a new replacement propeller I would ask to see the old one.

3. The gear oil in the lower leg.

4. The controls and gears.

5. The instruments and maybe the hour-meter if fitted.

6. The saddle bearings for excessive movement.

When buying secondhand I would recommend running the serial number back through the computer records held with the manufacturer. This will reveal when it was built. In my view 'I don't know when it was made, but it's quite new!' is a useless statement from the vendor. It is not unusual to find a secondhand boat being sold with an old and sometimes useless engine, the modern engine having been re-fitted onto a new hull. (If there is no serial number, be polite, say you will think about it and leave. You might also inform the police as thousands of outboards are stolen every year!)

Check the service history. If the engine has been serviced by a qualified engineer there should be a service record or supporting invoices, so do ask when it was last serviced.

Check for corrosion

If over five years old I would suggest that you should think twice before purchasing and find out if spares parts are still available. Check whether an engineer based in your area can look after it for you. This is essential if you are contemplating using the boat overseas as spares may prove difficult to find abroad.

When removing the hood the engine should be clean, free from corrosion and not hidden under large quantities of grease. If you're satisfied with the engine's condition, now is the time to review the whole boat in a similar way. Check the hull for damage and note how it is sitting and supported on the trailer rollers. It will be a matter of personal standards whether the condition of the seats, fabric and paintwork are acceptable to you.

Price

Ask the price and check how negotiable this figure is. Say you will be in touch. Be aware: remember that you will be told that there are at least two other people interested in the boat, and of course one will be returning with the cash in a couple of hours! Don't be rushed into panic buying.

While negotiating a purchase figure, I do recommend that you keep back a sum of money sufficient to cover a complete engine service before going to sea.

Compare prices in boating magazines selling similar boats. Telephone and/or visit several dealers.

It is difficult to make a generalised statement but it's often best to go for the boat which has been regularly used and maintained. I would avoid the boat which has only been worked for ten hours in the first week and then left standing for 36 months without use. The fact that it had not even had its first service is certainly no recommendation for its future reliability.

With a good boat and engine under you, the water beckons. See you out there!

Imagine using an outboard that isn't as

It's every boat owners' nightmare.

Your outboard breaks down in mid-channel and the barometer's falling. You can't just switch on the hazard warning lights and wait for the breakdown van, can you?

The best course is to fit a high performance Honda outboard engine in the first place. Their legendary reliability has been helping all kinds of craft steer clear of trouble for more than thirty years. All our models have four-stroke

* Subject to terms and conditions.

2HP

5HP

8HP

9.9HP

15HP

25HP

30HP

eliable as a Honda.

engines. So you won't have to worry about the plugs fouling up when you're idling. While superior fuel economy gives a cruising range with a comforting extra margin of safety. Starting is more reliable too. Honda outboards are also well known for their easy starting – very reassuring when storm clouds threaten. And remember that every Honda model comes with the option of a 5 year warranty for non-commercial users'. So next time you're choosing an outboard for your boat make sure it's a powerful Honda.

The alternative hardly bears thinking about.

40HP

50HP

75HP

90HP

Also by Peter White:

This book is the bible for all outboard craft. It covers launching and recovery, boat handling, manoeuvring at speed, rules of the road, mooring, tidal waters, charts, buoys and pilotage and man overboard. It explains how to use your boat for club rescue – eg for sailing dinghies and windsurfers. All with photo-sequences of the author in action.

Fernhurst Books publishes over eighty boating books.
If you would like a free full-colour brochure please write, phone or fax us:

Fernhurst Books,
Duke's Path, High Street, Arundel, West Sussex BN18 9AJ, England

Telephone: 01903 882277 Fax: 01903 882715